Anonymous

The Letters of Rabbi Akiba

the Jewish primer as it was used in the public schools two thousand years ago

Anonymous

The Letters of Rabbi Akiba

the Jewish primer as it was used in the public schools two thousand years ago

ISBN/EAN: 9783744718387

Printed in Europe, USA, Canada, Australia, Japan

Cover: Foto ©Lupo / pixelio.de

More available books at **www.hansebooks.com**

UNITED STATES BUREAU OF EDUCATION.

CHAPTER XIV FROM REPORT OF THE COMMISSIONER OF EDUCATION

FOR 1895-96.

THE LETTERS OF RABBI AKIBA,

OR

THE JEWISH PRIMER AS IT WAS USED IN THE PUBLIC
SCHOOLS TWO THOUSAND YEARS AGO.

WASHINGTON:
GOVERNMENT PRINTING OFFICE.
1897.

CHAPTER XIV.

THE LETTERS OF RABBI AKIBAH, OR THE JEWISH PRIMER AS IT WAS USED IN THE PUBLIC SCHOOLS TWO THOUSAND YEARS AGO.[1]

PREFACE BY THE COMMISSIONER OF EDUCATION.

This article is interesting and valuable in the history of education as showing the pains taken in Hebrew education to find a spiritual sense to all natural and artificial objects. Europeans and Americans are content to require their children to study the alphabet and master it as a mechanical affair. The Hebrew is of all peoples the one chosen by Divine Providence to ponder most carefully the spiritual sense of nature and human life. It would be expected, therefore, that an account of Hebrew education would show some of the devices by which the directive power of that wonderful people should manifest its sleepless care over the culture of the spiritual sense.

The lesson of the history of education of all peoples is this demonstration of the constant alertness, so to speak, of the national spirit in looking to its own preservation. The Chinese lay immense stress upon the mere verbal memory, teaching the etiquette laid down in the books of Confucius and Mencius. The child has all of his habits of thought trained in the direction of the observance of family etiquette. He learns to respect and obey his elder brother, his father and mother, and the officers of the State. He learns to protect those who depend in like manner upon him. This comes out in every phase of Chinese education. The culture peoples that have contributed to our civilization, the Greeks, the Romans, and the Jews, furnished still stronger illustrations of this principle. The Greeks contributed science and æsthetic art to modern civilization. The entire culture of the Greek people, at least of the Athenian people, has this significance. So, too, the Romans, who contributed to the world its sense of legal right, the protection of life and property. All that we learn about the Romans goes to give us an insight into the care which the spirit of the Roman people took to preserve in its education this insight into the human will, both the individual and the social will.

The student of the philosophy of history and the philosophy of education will read with interest this excerpt from the history of the Jewish education, as showing the neglect of what is mechanical and prosaic; what, in other words, is the letter for the spirit of it—the spiritual sense which the Hebrew mind finds underlying all objects in time and space.

HISTORY AND NATURE OF THE PRIMER.

When I was engaged in writing the first part of my treatise on Hebrew education I discovered an ancient Jewish text-book, which was written for the public schools by the great educator Rabbi Akibah, who lived at the time of the second destruction. When I mentioned my discovery to the well-known scholar Hon. Judge Mayer

---

[1] Discovered and translated for the first time by Prof. Naphtali Herz Imber, 1896.

Sulzberger, of Philadelphia, he encouraged me to examine the booklet more carefully. A careful investigation followed, and I found it to be an ancient Jewish primer. The booklet contains about sixty small printed pages, written in fine classic Hebrew. Its antiquity is soon recognized by its spiritual tendency. The composition is made on the same principle as that of the Alpha Bethical picture book of the ancient Jewish primary school, namely: It is built on the letters of the Hebrew Alpha Beth. While the letters of the Alpha Beth were explained to the children, the meanings of their figures, shapes, and positions, this Jewish primer endeavors to explain the letters and meanings of the terms.

The tablets in the primary school correspond more to our modern picture books, while the Jewish primer has the character and poetical touch of modern readers. The booklet is divided into three parts; the first is of a lighter matter than the second, and the second than the third. It is probable that the first part was made for the first school standard, while the second and third portions were calculated for the higher classes. The third part assumes the character of theological commentaries. In general, it breathes a deep religious, poetical, spiritual tone, and we can now understand the psychological problem how the Hebrews, whose religion was void of the idealistic charm which characterized the religion of the Pagans, yet proved to be better devotees to their faith in spite of its dryness and lack of inspiring motives. The answer to that problem is the Jewish primer, and the idealistic spiritual education which was implanted in the heart of the child by it, and has inspired later the grown Hebrew to endure temptations, as well as persecution. From a historical and educational point of view the Jewish primer is of great value, bearing testimonies to the great power of education.

THE TRANSLATION.

FIRST PART.

Said Rabbi Akibah, those are the twenty-two letters, by and through which the "Torah" (the law) was given to all the tribes of Israel. They are engraved by a fairy pen upon the most exalted crown of the Holy One; praise to Him. When the will of the Holy One was to create the universe, those letters arrayed themselves before the Lord, each desiring to be made the medium of the creative force. First appeared the Taw, the last of the letters in the Alpha Beth, and begged that the Lord would create the world with it, pleading "O Lord, create through me the world as I am the first letter of the Torah (the law)." The Lord then replied, "No." Then the Taw asked why, and the Lord answered, "Because I will put thee as a sign of destruction upon the foreheads of the wicked." Taw means a sign in Hebrew as it is written in Ezekiel (xvi), and the Lord said unto me, "Pass through Jerusalem, and put a sign upon the foreheads of the groaning and moaning people for the iniquities they did." What is the meaning of the sign? When the Almighty resolved to destroy Jerusalem He called to the Angel of Death, saying unto him, "Go through Jerusalem and divide the wicked and the good ones. Upon the former make a Taw of blood, a sign of death, while upon the latter sign a Taw of ink, the symbol of life." Why is the shape of the Taw peculiar from all the letters? Because the Torah saves man from all troubles. At that time the Spirit of Justice appeared before the Lord, urging the destruction of the good ones too. The Lord asked why, and the Spirit of Justice replied, " Because they did not warn the wicked." The Lord replied, "It is known to me that those wicked would not heed their warnings." Then the Spirit of Justice said that it was their duty to warn regardless of the consequences. The Lord then declared that they should share the same fate as the wicked.

At that time six destructive angels were sent upon Jerusalem to destroy her people, as it is written (Ezekiel ix), "Behold, six men were coming from the upper gate, facing the north side, each armed, and the man dressed in linen stood among them, and the pen of a writer on his loins, and he went near the copper altar." Why the north side? Because all ill winds are blowing only from the north side, as it is written (Jeremiah i) "And he said unto me, from the north the ill fate will come upon the dwellers of the land." As soon as the Taw heard it from the mouth of the Most High the latter left the place sorrowful.

Then appeared before the Lord the letter Shin, the next to the last of the letters, praying the Lord to create with it the world, under the plea that the letter Shin is the first letter in the Holy Name of Shadi (the Almighty). Then the Lord refused to accept on the ground that Shin is the first letter of falsehood, "Sheker." "And how," said the Lord, "can I create the world with a letter which has no foot? and falsehood has no footing." The Shin went out sorrowful, and the letter Reish appeared before the Lord with the same wish, saying, "I am the first letter of Thy name, the Merciful and the Healer." But the Lord said "No, as Reish is the first letter of Rashu, which means wicked." So the Reish left sorrowful, and the K appeared before the Lord, asking that the world may be created with it, as the people will praise the Lord with that letter in saying thrice Holy, Holy, Holy, is the Lord Zebaath (Kadosh means holy). The Lord refused on the ground that curse is prepared to come over the generations of the flood, and in Hebrew curse is "Kellala." The K went out sorrowful, and the Zadic or Z appeared before the Lord with the same wish as the former letters, saying, "Create with me the world, as Thou art called Zadic" (Righteous One). The Lord refused and said "No, as many troubles are to come with thee upon Israel" (Zara is trouble in Hebrew). The Z went out sorrowful, and the P came before the Lord, saying, "Create with me the world, as the laws will be called Pikiddim, and I am the first letter in Thy name as Redeemer" (Pode is redeemer in Hebrew). The Lord replied "No, as they will serve the idols with thee" (Peor is the famous name of a famous idol). The P went out sorrowful, and the E or Ain came before the Lord, saying, "Create with me the world, as it is written (Zachazje) the eyes of the Lord are upon the whole universe" (Ain is eye in Hebrew). The Lord replied "No, as with thee the people watch the night, to commit crime and sin, as it is written (Job xxiv) 'the eye of the adulterer watches the night, and I will punish the wicked by thee,' as it is written (Job xi) 'the eyes of the wicked will go out.'" The E went out sorrowful, and the S or Samech came before the Lord, saying, "Create with me the world, as through me Thou art called the leaner of the fallen ones" (Samech is leaning). The Lord said "No, as with thee the pagans will destroy my city, as it is written (Psalms) 'they made Jerusalem the ruins of piles.'" The S went out, and the N or Nun came before the Lord, saying, "Create with me the world, as with me Thou willst resurrect the dead, and I am called the candle of the Lord, which is the soul in man" (Proverbs xx). ("Ner" is candle.) The Lord answered "No, as I will blow out the light of the wicked in the latter days to come." The N went out sorrowful, and the M or Mim came before the Lord saying, "Create with me the world, as with me the generations to come will crown Thee proclaiming Thy Heavenly, Eternal Kingdom, and with me Thou art called King (Melech)." The Lord said "No, as with thee will come a day of compassion." The M went out sorrowful, and the L or Lamed came before the Lord, saying, "Create with me the world, as with me Thou wilt once give to Israel the two tablestones, and Israel will learn Thy laws." (Lamed means study.) The Lord said "No, as the tablestones will be broken." The L went out sorrowful, and the Caf came before the Lord. At that hour, when the Caf went down from the Crown divine (Keter is crown), a storm arose in the celestial realm. When the Caf appeared before the glorious throne, the throne began to be shaken, and the wheels of the glorious chariot began to tremble. The Lord inquired for their uneasiness, and they said, "For the Caf went down from the exalted glorious crown of our heads and stays before Thee, and all our glory is only called by the Caf, as it is written (Jeremiah xvii), 'Exalted glorious throne, the glory of God is forever.'" So the Lord called to the Caf, saying, "What is thy wish?" The Caf said, "O Lord of the universe, create with me the world, as with me is named Thy Throne, Thy Glory, and Thy Crown." He answered "No, as by thee I will once clutch with my hands for grief, as it is written (Ezekiel xxi) 'I will too clutch my hands (Caf is hand); with thee will also go out the tears of my people and I shall create with thee the world.'" The C went out sorrowful, and the Jod came before the Lord, saying, "O Lord, create with me the world, as with me Thou art named Ja the Creator of the Worlds" (Isaiah xxvi). The Lord said, "No, as with thee I will create the wicked thought in man to lure him away from the good path." The Jod went out sorrowful, and the T or Teth came before the Lord, saying, "O Lord, create with me the world, as with me Thou willst send the Holy Ghost to those who fear Thee, and in me is hidden the good one" (Tob is good). The Lord said "No, as with thee I will once call my people 'unclean,' 'Tame,' and every leper will be so called." The T went out sorrowful, and the Ch or Cheth came before the Lord, saying, "O Lord, create with me the world, as with me they feel Thy mercy feeling the whole universe, and with me Thou art called merciful." The Lord said "No, as with thee I once will engrave with an iron pen the sin of Judah." The Ch went out sorrowful, and the S or Sain came before the Lord, saying, "O Lord, create with me the world, as Thy reverence from generation to generation exists with me." The Lord said "No, as adultery will come upon the world through thee, and as a consequence Israel will lose twenty-four thousand people, and how can I create the world with thee?" The S went out sorrowful, and the W or Waw came before the Lord, saying, "O Lord, create with me the world, as with me they praise Thee, Thou Holy One in Israel." The Lord said, "No, as I once will inflict upon Israel for their passions." The W went out sorrowful, and the H or He came before the Lord, saying, "O Lord, create with me the world, as with me they acknowledge Thy majesty and glory." The Lord answered, "No, as with thee I will once in the later days of judgment make the day that of penance, burning all the wicked and evil doers." The H went out sorrowful, and the D or Dalith came before the Lord, saying, "O Lord, create with me the world, as with me the generations will exalt Thee, as it is written (Psalms cxlviii) 'Generation to generation will praise Thy work.'" The Lord answered, "No, as with thee Israel will experience judgment among themselves, as it is written in the Scripture." The D went out sorrowful, and the G or Gimel came before the Lord, saying, "O Lord, create with me the world, as with me the people praise Thy greatness." The Lord answered "No, as with thee I will pay to the enemies, as it is written (Isaiah lix) 'as to the reward He will pay.'" The G went out sorrowful, and the B or Beth came before the Lord, saying, "O Lord, create with me the world, as with me all the creation praises Thy glorious name, as it is written (Psalms lxxxix), 'Blessed be the Lord forever; Amen. Praise the Lord all His hosts. All the coming generations will say, Blessed be the Lord God of Israel and Blessed be the glorious name forever'" (Psalms lxxvi). The B is the first letter in Hebrew for blessed. As soon as the Lord heard the plea of the B he accepted, and created the world with the letter B as it is written in Genesis. "Breishith Bara Elohim," which means with B created the Lord heaven and earth. As the A or the Aleph heard and saw how the Lord had accepted the letter B it went aside meditating in silence. Then the Lord said unto the A, "Why art thou silent?" and the A replied, "Because I do not count for much, as I represent only number one, while the other letters represent much, as B, number two, C, three, D, four, and so on." Then the Lord said, "Be not afraid, as thou art the king over all the letters; thou art one, and I am one, and the law is one, and with thee I will give it to Israel, my people, who are called one (nation), as the first letter of the Ten Commandments is the A or Aleph in the word 'Anochi' 'I am thy Lord.'"[1]

---

[1] The pleadings of the letters in every sentence they mention is that each letter begins the respective Biblical passage. The way of its composition shows the childish spirit, yet in that most fantastic tale is hidden one thought of the most prevalent philosophy of that age—the Logos idea.

AN ANCIENT JEWISH PRIMER. 705

SECOND PART.

Why is the head of the A or Aleph upright standing on two legs as men? Because it is second in Truth (A is the first letter of Emeth, truth) and falsehood has no legs to stand upon, since all the letters of falsehood have no foothold. Why is his hand stretched out from his side? Because he shows to the Almighty, who is Truth Himself, as it is written (Psalm cxvi) "and the Truth of the Lord forever."

Why is the B or Beth with its open face toward the G? Because the B resembles a house (Beth is house in Hebrew) open to all, and the G resembles a man who sees a poor one at the door, and goes into the house to bring out some food.

Why is the foot of the G or Gimel toward the D? Because all mercy must be extended to the poor. (Dal is poor in Hebrew.)

Why is the D or Dalith resembling a stick and facing the H? Because the poor man is striving only for the bliss of the material world.

Why is the H or Hei resembling an open hut? Because he who wants to get out of it can do so. Why has it two doors, one small and one large? Because he who wants to get out goes out through the larger, and he who wants to get in must come in through the smaller. (Allegory for birth and death.)

Why is the W or Waw upright like a stick facing the S? Because God has hinted through the symbols of the letters that He will once punish the wicked by messengers with fire sticks of the purgatory, from where their woe cry will be heard, as it is written (Isaiah iii) "Woe to the wicked."

Why has the S or Sain two points on its head, one toward the Waw and the other the Cheth? Because if one goes to sin, he looks twice, once to be hidden from men, the other look is directed toward the crime.

Why has the Ch or Chet no crown? Because the wicked have only shame, and they are void of good name. (Chet means sin.)

Why is the hand of the T or Teth hidden inside and its head upright with a crown on? Because he who does good and helps the poor that nobody sees will calm the wrath even that of the Angel of Death, as it is written (Proverbs xxi) "A hidden gift calms the wrath."

Why is the Jod smaller than all the letters? Because he who humbles himself here will inherit the life hereafter, which was created with that letter. Why is the point of it toward its face? Because each one gets rewarded according to his merit, and his good deeds are before him.

Why resembles the Caf a throne and facing the L? Because a throne is fit only for the kings to sit on. (Kese is throne, and Melech is king.)

Why is the L or Lamed taller than all the letters? Because it stands in the center of the twenty-two letters, and resembles a king, a throne behind and kingdom before him.

Why is there an open M and a close M? (The former is used in the middle of the word as well as at the beginning, while the latter only at the end.) Because there is an open king and there is a close king. Why is the head of the open M toward the ground with the hand stretched on high? Because it points out to Him, to whom all kingdom belongs, as it is written (Psalm xxii) "To Thee, O Lord, is the Kingdom," and at the same time looks to the ground to show, as King David said, "From Thee is all." The closed M points out that all is closed to us.

Why is the N or Nun facing the S or Samech? Because it looks as one who falls and prays to be leaned.

Why is the S or Samech closed around? Because it is a symbol to Israel, who is closed round on all the corners with divine glory, and that He will not exchange him for another nation, and his seed will not be mixed with the seed of others, as it is written "The Lord belongs to His people." Also it is written (Zechariah) "I, the Lord, will surround thee with a fire wall."

The E or Ain is the initial of Esau the wicked, from whom Persians and Tarsians

ED 96——23

came forth. Why is the E in a sitting position? Because they will fall before the feet of Israel, as it is written (Obadja i) "The house of Jacob will be fire and Edom will be his inheritance."
Why is there a sitting and a standing P? (The standing P is only used at the end of a word.) Because the mouth which opens the same seals. (P means mouth.) The idol worshipers have no open mouth in the laws and in the oral law or in prayers; only Israel alone, as it is written (Psalms cxlvii) "He told His words to Jacob. He did not so to any nation."
Why has the Z or Zadic two heads? Because there are two kinds of righteous people; the one plain and the other with humility.
Why is the K or Kaf tall and horned? Because all the horns of the wicked will be cut off, for they walk proudly in this life. As it is written (Psalm lxxviii) "And all the horns of the wicked I will cut off." He will again exalt those of Israel, as it is written (Psalm lxxv) "Exalted will be the horns of the pious ones."
Why is the face of the R or Reish turned away from the K? Because R is the initial of the wicked, and K the initial of the holy, and the wicked is always turning away from the holy.
Why has the Sch or Shin three branches above and no foot or root below? Because the Shin is the initial of falsehood, and falsehood has no foothold and the Almighty will stop the mouth of falsehood. It resembles a tree whose branches are plentiful and the roots little; the wind can easily turn it over.
Why is the foot of the Taw a little broken up? Because Taw is the initial of the Torah, the law, and he who wants to study the law must humble and lower himself.

ANOTHER EXPLANATION FOR THE ALPHA BETH.

Aleph Beth means, learn wisdom. (Aleph means learn; Beth is like Bina wisdom, and on that line the whole Alpha Beth is explained according to the meanings of their terms.)
Gimmel Dalith means, be merciful to the poor. Why is the leg of the Gimel stretched forward? Because the good ones are apt after the poor to help them. Why is the back of the Dalith turned toward the Gimel? Because the poor looks behind him expecting somebody to help him.
Why is the H after D? Because he who helps the poor will become great.
Why is the W after H? Because of him who does not help the poor, they say, "Woe to that man who can but will not do good with his wealth," and it is written (Proverbs xi) "He who keeps away his wealth from charity, will lose it."
Why come after WS and S Ch? They show that if one have conquered his temper and done good, then he will find mercy at the throne of the Almighty.
Why are the letters of truth scattered and the letters of falsehood together. (A is the initial of Emeth, truth; M is the second letter, and Taw is the last letter, while Sheker, falsehood, formed from the letters Sh, k, r, are following each other.) Because truth is very rare to find, while falsehood is behind the ear. As they taught in the College of Rabbi Ismael, he who wants to become impure, they open to him, but he who tries to be pure, they help him.
Why are the five special letters of double character? (There are five letters in the Hebrew Alpha Beth which have double ones, and they are used at the end of the words; they are M, N, Z, P, Ch.)
The simple Caf and the closed Caf show the simple hand of Moses and the closed hand of God.
The open M and the closed M show that there is an open sentence (or word) and a hidden word, and from it must be learned the good manner; that the teacher shall speak and the pupil silent and listening.
The bowed Z and the simple Z; the former represents the bowed pious one, the latter the simple one. Each sage must study and seek the truth of the law with

the utmost sincerity, as it is written (Psalm cxv) "Hail to those who keep His law; with all their hearts they seek Him."[1]

THIRD PART.

"At" "Bash." Aleph is Adam, who was the first creature of the world, as the creation was created by the word (logos), but he was created by the hand of the Almighty. How do I know that the world was created by the word? Then it is written (Psalm xxxiii), "He said, and it was;" in another line he says, "By the word of God the Heavens were made."

How do I know that Adam was made by His hand? As it is written (Genesis) "And the Lord created the man." What is the meaning of the passsage (Psalm cxxxix) "And Thou puttest Thy hand upon me?" The Lord made first Adam so tall that his height was from the ground to the sky. When the angels saw him they began to tremble and appeared before the Lord saying, "Are there two Lords; one in Heaven and the other on earth?" What did God? He simply put his hand on him and shortened his height 2,000 cubits.

Bash, B, is the initial of animals. Shin is the initial of reptiles, which were created with Adam. Why have they been created with him? Because the Lord says, "If he gets proud, then we say to him, Behold, animals and reptiles were created as you, too."

Gar Dack (a combination of the letter G with R, and the letter D with K, and so goes on through the whole order of the Alpha Beth). Gar, Gimel; this represents the Garden of Eden, placing there twelve canopies of precious stones and of pearls for Adam, as it is written (Ezechiel xxv) "In Eden the Garden of the Lord thou wast: all the precious stones were thy shelter." R means that he, Adam, went the first into Eden before all the pious ones.

D, K. D means the doors of Eden, which angels opened to him, whom the Lord appointed as his servants. K means holy; these angels called him Adam, "holy."

H, Z. H as the Almighty lulled Adam into sleep. Z means the rib which He took from him to form from it his counterpart, his wife.

W, F. W means that He brought Eve to Adam, accompanied by tens of thousands of angels, who were singing and cheering. F means that the whole celestial family went down into Eden; some of them were playing on harps and the others play instruments, playing like virgins; while sun, moon, and stars were dancing before them as girls.

S, E. S means that the Lord invited them both to a banquet in Eden. E means that the Lord prepared for them tables of pearl; each pearl was 2 cubits long and 60 cubits broad, and all sorts of food were thereon, as it is written (Psalm xxiii) "'Thou preparest a table for me."

Ch, S. Ch means that the angels did servant duty, roasting his meat and cooling his wine, and the serpent saw their honor and envied them. S means that the Lord told him not to eat from the tree of knowledge.

[1] The second part was, judging from its character, probably taught in the next school standard calculated for pupils from 8 to 10 years old. The second part does not contain the childish fantasy heated by the steam of oriental imagination. It simply explains the letters of the Alpha Beth in the line of their words and terms, while at the same time it tries to implant in the heart of the child religious, moral, and national patriotic sentiments. The third part is in quantity as well as quality far superior to the other two, for it has a homiletic character, and tries to make the child acquainted with some of the most truly national and religious traditions and legends. A new mode of explaining the letters is, that it takes the first letter of the Alpha Beth, combines with the last Taw and forms a new word "At," which is explained by some folklore.

Then it takes the next letter B combining with the next last letter Sh or Shin and a word "Bash" is formed and explained. That way was for training the child's brain to the scholastic way of argument among the sages of the Rabbis of the Talmud. The gradual rising of the thought in the primer indicates the great educational principle which the author had before his eyes. The third part of the primer was for pupils of the age of 10 and upward: it was calculated to prepare them for the study of the Talmud and oral law.

F, N. F means that Eve mistook the words of the serpent, and ate from the forbidden fruit. N means that their eyes were opened to see that they were naked, and they covered their nakedness with fig leaves.

Jod, M. Yod means that the Almighty was aware of it, and he went down to call Adam for it. M means that the Lord questioned him, "Who told you that you were naked?"

C, L. C means that the Lord invited them all for judgment. First, He called aside Adam, asking him why he ate from the fruit. Adam defended himself, saying that Eve gave him to eat. The woman was questioned, and she pleaded that she did it under the temptation of the serpent. The serpent was called and cursed. When the Lord said to the serpent "On thy belly thou shalt go," the serpent begged, "O Lord, make me as the fish in water, which have no feet," and the Lord said, "Dust shall be thy food." Then the serpent said, "If the fish eat dust, I will eat it too." At that moment the Lord tore his tongue in two parts, saying, "Wicked one, thou hast sinned in gossip, since I make known to the world that it is on account of thy unruly tongue."

A, Ch, S, means that God said unto the angels, I, myself, will be more merciful to Israel than to the idol worshipers, for the former crown me twice a day and proclaim my kingdom morning and evening by their declarations, "Hear, O Israel, the Lord our God is one." If Israel would not exist, neither glory nor exaltation would exist.

B, T, E (Bata). My spirit is only calmed by Israel, for the heathen make mistakes to take sun, moon, and stars as deities. And when they bow before them and before the hosts of Heaven, then the Holy One is wrath, as it is written (Psalm vii), "God is wrath every day." The Almighty says unto the angels, "Behold, I gave unto those pagans spirit, mind, glory, and ruling power, and they bow to sun, moon, and stars, which I have created from the aureole of my face." At that saying they tremble, those wheels in the orbits of the sun, moon, and stars, and two destructive angels go out to destroy the world on account of their wicked doings, but they give up their intention for the sake of the sages who study the law, and the public-school children who read the scripture, and for the sake of the whole of Israel who proclaim morning and evening the Heavenly Kingdom.

G, I, F. (Gif), do not read Gif only Guf, body, that is the body of the Torah, that the teachers of the colleges are trying to explain to Israel as it is written, "They will teach thy laws to Jacob."

D, Ch, Z. (Dachaz), do not read Dachaz only "Dach Kulu Chefez," meaning the humble one is the whole longing. The pious ones are the "land of desire" of God. Why are the pious ones called "desire?" Because they fulfill the desire of the Almighty.

Ch. L. K. (Cheleck), meaning part that is Jacob, who is the property of the Lord, as the glorious name was sanctified through him and his children, and the Lord has engraved his image on his glorious throne. When the children of Jacob say thrice a day praise to God, then the Lord kisses his head, which is engraved upon His glorious throne.

How do I know that Jacob is the property of God? Then it is written the property of God is his people, Jacob the property of his inheritance.

N. M. R. (Nmar), meaning "he said;" those are the seraphim and fairy angels who can not say praise to the glory of the Lord, until Israel has first sanctified his holy name, as it is written (Job xxxviii) "The morning stars sing together and the sons of God shout for joy." The morning stars are the children of Israel, as Moses said, and ye are as the stars of the sky. As the stars are shining, so the children of Israel are shining through the light of the law, as it is written (Proverbs vi), "The good deed is a candle and the law is light."

S, N. (Son) Sh, T, (Shot) are the initials of the words, "He bears the Sabbath." When God promised Israel the pleasures of life hereafter in exchange for keeping the laws, Israel demanded a sample of that pleasure, and the Lord gave him the Sabbath.

When Nagrasniel, the manager of the Purgatory, asked the Lord, "Why didst thou not give me that nation of Israel as food for my flames as others?" the Lord replied, "All the pagans are written in thy books, with the exception of Israel, as they study the law, and I am with them." He then asked, "Where will they live in life hereafter?" And the Lord answered, "In the garden of Eden, full of myrrh and spices, whose fragrant air penetrates from one corner of the world to the other." Then he wanted to know how they would enjoy their glorious time, and the Almighty will say, "With me does not dwell the wicked. Israel will once, in the later days, be void of the tempting wicked thought, and neither Satan nor the Angel of Death will approach their dwellings."

Then Nagrasniel will ask, "O Lord, Thou givest everyone his daily bread, give me also," and the Lord will say, "I have given you all the wicked of the land, liars, and the gossipers and worshipers and the evil doers."

IN PRAISE OF MUSIC.

Said Rabbi Akibah, Aleph is the initial of, Truth, learn thy mouth. Tell truth in order to have a share in life hereafter. God is truth; His throne is truth, and He receives the truth. His words are truth, His ways are truth, and His laws are truth. As it is written in the Scriptures, Jehovah Elohim is truth. (Jeremiah x.) Aleph is the initial of the words, I will open mouth and tongue. Said the Holy, praise Him! I will open the mouths of the children of flesh and blood that they shall praise me every day, and proclaim my kingdom into all the corners of the universe. If it had not been for the sake of song and music, which they exercise for me every day, I would not have created my universe.[1]

How do we know that God created the world only for the sake of music and song? Then it is written (Psalm xcvi), "Majesty and beauty before Him, might and glory in His temple, and of His praise is the earth full." That God has made the heavens only for the sake of music, as it is written (Psalm xix), "The heavens declare the glory of God." That we know, that the earth sings since she was created, for it is written (Isaiah, xxiv), "From the corner (or border) of the earth we hear a song to the righteous, and only God is righteous," as it is written (Psalm cxlv), "God is righteous in all his ways." How do we know that even seas and streams sing to the Almighty? For it is written (Psalm cxlviii), "Praise the Lord, all the heavens, and the water." Even all the creation praises the Lord with music and song. Even Adam opened his mouth with song. (It is a Talmudical legend that Adam was the author of the ninety-second chapter of the Psalms.) I will open mouth and tongue, as among the two hundred and forty-eight parts of the human body (pretty near to our modern teaching of anatomy) with none of them is it so fit to praise the Lord as with mouth and tongue.

Mouth and tongue can be compared only to the ocean and its waves. As the ocean opens ajar, so the mouth. As the ocean is full of pearls, so the mouth (alluding to the teeth). As the ocean brings forth the water, so the mouth. As the wave is lifting itself high, so the tongue. As the ocean destroys a ship, so the tongue destroys with a word. As the ocean roars, so the mouth. As the waves kill the people, so the tongue kills people. As the ocean has borders, so the mouth has borders. As the ocean is sometimes calm and sometimes stormy, so the mouth. As all fear the waves, so all fear the human tongue. As the outlet of the waters of the ocean turns to filth, so the words of the mouth turn into nothingness. God said (so runs another version), "I will open the mouth of Israel to praise my name every day, for nothing is pure in the world without Israel and music, as for their sakes the world exists, and I created Israel only for the sake of song, as it is written (Isaiah xliv), 'My nation I created my praise to tell.'"

---

[1] Here we see plainly how the primer or its author tried to implant into the hearts of the children the love of music.—The translator.

If there is no Aleph, then there is no Beth, meaning if there is no learning there is no house. If there is no G there is no D, meaning if there is no charity there is no poor, and if there is no poor there is no charity. Israel is called poor, as it is written (Psalm xviii), "Thou helpest the poor nation, and the eyes of the proud ones, those of the heathen, thou makest down."

Another version of the initial of the Aleph is that God says, "My truth I have deposited by Israel." When God gave the law to Israel, he promised them the pleasure of future life in exchange for keeping the law. Israel demanded a sample of that pleasure and the Lord gave them the Sabbath. How do we know that the Sabbath is a prototype of future life? For it is written (Psalm xcii), "A song to the day of Sabbath," meaning the life hereafter which is an everlasting Sabbath.

When Adam saw the Sabbath he began to sing the praise of the Holy One. At that moment the angels went down in parties, some played instruments and others different kinds of musical works, praising, singing and saying "God," as it is written (Psalm), "To sing to the name of the Most High, to tell at the mornings Thy mercy, and at nights Thy truth."

The mornings means future life, and nights this life, as it is written (Psalm civ), "Thou makest darkness and there is night, there the beasts of the forest are roaming." Do the beasts only roam at night, and not at day too?

But it is alluding to this life which is as dark as night, and the idol worshipers which resemble the beasts who roam in the forest at night. When the morning star dawns the beasts turn into their dens, so when the morning of the Messiah's kingdom will dawn the heathen will turn back, never to come into life hereafter, as it is written, "God will be the King of the universe."

Aleph means thousand; five thousand gates of wisdom has the Lord opened to Moses, corresponding to his five books. Eight thousand gates of "knowledge" corresponding to the eight prophets, and eleven thousand gates of higher wisdom corresponding to the eleven books of Scripture (those of Ruth and the like). As it is written (Proverbs xxi), "A desirable treasure and oil is the dwelling of the sage." A treasure is the law, oil is the books of the scripture, calming man like balmy oil.

Another version of the Aleph is representing the Holy One. As the Aleph is the first of all the letters so is God the first of all the kings, and He is also the last of the nobles, as it is written (Isaiah 11) "I the Lord am first, and with the last ones, I am." Why is it written with the last ones, and not with the last one? From it we learn that when God renews His world He himself arranges the order of the last ones, the order of the pious, the order of the righteous, the order of the humble ones, the order of the prophets, the order of kings, of princes, of nobility, of generations, the order of every being, the order of every beast and bird, and that of every soul. Those arranged in order, He brings down Enoch, the son of Jered, whose proper name is "Mettatron," and the four holy beasts from under the wheels of His glorious throne, and places His throne on one side. Then He brings up Korah and his gang from the depth of the purgatory. Then He brings forth all the living visitors of this life, placing them on their legs. Then He asks them, "Did ye ever see a God like me, either in heaven above or on earth beneath, or in any of the four corners of the world? Be witness unto me, and say the truth," as it is written (Isaiah 43) "Ye are my witness that I am God!" Then Mettatron and the holy beasts with Korah and his gang will say in one voice, "We never saw a God like Thee, neither in Heaven above nor on earth below; Thou art the first and last, and no other God except Thee, our Lord and King," as it is written (Psalm 86) "There is no God like Thee and none as Thy work."

At that hour the Lord will reply, "Verily, I, I am and no God with me. I was before I created the world and I am with the creation, and I will be a God in life hereafter. I kill and I will resurrect, I wounded them in this life and will heal them in future life. With the same fault with which he parts from this life, with the same he will appear at the resurrection—the blind, the lame, the deaf, and the kindred afflicted beings. And the Lord will sit as a healer and heal them."

Why is Aleph written as one letter and read as a syllable of three letters. Because it represents the Holy One who is one, and the reading of his name is a threefold, as it is written "Hear Israel, (1) God our, (2) Lord, (3) God is one." His praise and sanctification is also a threefold, as it is written "Holy, holy, holy is the Lord Zebaath." Even the song is a threefold as the song of songs of Solomon. Song is one, songs are two, here is a threefold song.[1]

Seventy names has the Holy One, those of the known ones, while the unknown are numberless.

Aleph is the initial of "have chosen," "have taken," "have appointed." Said the Lord, all those are applied to Mettatron my servant, who is sublimer than all the celestials. Have chosen him in Adam's generation, when the generation of the flood got wicked, and took away my glory from them (in the text is "my Shechina," meaning the divine womanhood), and went to the heavens amid the blowing of the horns, as it is written (Psalm 47), "God went on high by the voice of the horns." Then I selected Enoch, the son of Jered, from them, to be with me a living witness with the four holy beasts in my chariot. I appointed him on all my treasures in my celestial realm, and the keys of them I handed over to him. I made him a prince of princes to the glorious throne, a manager to four holy beasts, and to put crowns on their heads.

I made his height higher than all the celestial beings, 7,000 miles taller. I exalted his throne from mine. I turned his body into a flame and his bones into glittering light. I made his appearance as the appearance of lightning, his eyes as the eternal light, and the reflection of his face as the reflection of the sun, the rays of his eyes as the rays of the glorious throne, his garment of majesty and beauty. I crowned him with a crown 500 miles on 500 miles measure, and gave from my majesty to him.

I called him in my name "Jedud the Little," who knows all the secrets and mysteries which I revealed unto him in love. I placed his throne at the entrance of my palace, to do judgment among the celestial family. Seventy names I named him in order to increase his glory. Seventy princes I placed under him in order to execute through them the fates of existence, to uplift the lowly and to make low the proud ones, to smite the kings with his word and to humiliate the nobles, to alter the run of time and to reveal wisdom to the earthly kings, delivering the secrets to those who strive for knowledge. That Mettatron sits in Heaven three hours each day, gathering round him all those souls of infants, sucklings, and of school children who died before their times. He gathers them under the glorious throne, dividing them in divisions and sections, and teaches them the law, wisdom and knowledge, and all the secrets of the Torah, as it is written (Isaiah 28), "To whom will he teach wisdom, to whom will he explain the tidings? To those who were deprived from milk, taken from off the breasts."

THE PRINCE OF WISDOM.

Sagnasel is the Prince of Wisdom. Why is his name Sagnasal? Because the treasures of wisdom are given into his hand. All those treasures were opened to Moses while on Mount Sinai, where Sagnasel taught him the law in seventy languages and in seventy ways. The prophets, the oral laws, and all knowledge pertaining to religion he taught him in seventy ways. At the expiration of his forty days Moses forgot all in one hour, and the Holy One called upon Jefeifia, the prince of the law, and presented him as a gift to Moses, and then his memory was strengthened. Those ninety-two names of the Holy One, names of the outspoken name,

---

[1] The following chapter must have been for the last standard of the grammar school. Its mystical environment, its more completed narratives, indicated the character and purpose of that portion of the "reader." The so oft-cited sentences of the Scripture were probably calculated to impress the pupil with the idea that the Bible is the source of all knowledge, training him to study and to know it by heart.

which are engraved upon the glorious throne, which the Holy One gave from His name to Mettatron, and the twenty-two seals by which all the celestial orders are sealed, also the books of kings and of angels, of the Grim Messenger, and the books of fate of every nation.

Said Mettatron, the prince of the interior, the prince of the law, the prince of wisdom, the prince of glory, the prince of the palace, the prince of the angels, the prince of princes above and below, that the Lord, the God of Israel is my witness, that when I revealed that secret to Moses there arose an uproar among the celestial hosts, and they protested. They said to me, "Why do you reveal that secret to the sons of man, born from a woman, who are full of faults, unclean, full of blood and disease? Why do you reveal that secret by which the creation was called into existence, why do you reveal to man of flesh and blood?" I replied to them, "Because I took a permit from the Holy One. Therefore I revealed to him the meanings of the names going out from light and fire." They were not satisfied with my explanations, and the Lord said, "I want so, and I appointed Mettatron alone, and he can give it to Moses." Moses delivered that to Jehoshua, and Jehoshua to the elders, and the elders to the prophets, the prophets to the men of the great synod, and the great synod to Ezra the scribe, and Ezra to Hillel the Great, and Hillel to Rab Ahluhn, and Rab Ahluhn to the men of faith (the Essenes), and the men of faith to the people of religions to take care of it, and to heal by it all the diseases, as it is written, if thou hear and keep the words of the Lord I will not bring upon thee the plagues I brought down upon Egypt, as I, thy God, am thy healer.

B reads as Beth, which means a house (the initials of Beth). Said the Lord, I builded, I formed, I prepared, I builded my two palaces, one in Heaven and the other on earth. I formed all the orders of creation. I prepared the future life.

Why has God created the world with the letter B? Because the Lord knew that the world would be twice destroyed, once by the generation of the flood and once at the end of 6093 years since the creation. (The letter B is in Hebrew No. 2.)

Another reason, as the temple will be destroyed twice. For he created two worlds, life here and life to come. For God said, I created two palaces, one for me and the other for the sons of man, as it is written (Psalms), "Heaven belongs to the Lord, the earth he gave to the sons of man."

Said the Holy One, for the people will have two kinds of worship, Israel will worship me, the pagans, idols. Another reason, because the people have a dual thought, one good and the other evil.

Three are called "first," the Torah, Israel, and the fear of the Lord, and for their sake the world was created. By the Torah is written (Proverbs 14), "The Lord bought me, the first of His way." "Israel," as it is written (Jeremiah), "holy is Israel to the Lord, the first of his fruit." Fear of the Lord is also called "first," as it is written (Proverbs 1), "The first of wisdom is the fear of the Lord."

B is Binda, knowledge or understanding. Without understanding the world could not exist even one hour, as it is written (Deuteronomy), "Select from you men of wisdom and understanding." When God requested Moses to select men of understanding to make them tribal leaders, Moses went throughout all the camps of Israel to seek for men of understanding, and he could not find them.

Understanding is dearer to the Almighty than the Torah; if a man knows all the laws of the Torah, all the scripture, all the knowledge, and has not the understanding, he has nothing acquired.

G is the initial of Charity. If there was no charity the world could not exist. The Lord said, If it had not been for my charity the world could not exist. What is the charity that God does to this world daily? It consists in giving the people spirit, wisdom, understanding, thought, power, light of the eyes, hearing of the ears, motion of the feet, feeling of the hands, the opening of the mouths, and the talk of the tongue. As it is written (Psalm 33), "The charity of the Lord is full on the earth." Spirit and soul, as it is written that the Lord blew into his nostrils a living

AN ANCIENT JEWISH PRIMER. 713

breath. Wisdom, as it is written, "The Lord gives from this mouth wisdom and knowledge." The sense of hearing, as it is written, "And the ears of the deaf will be opened." Walk of the legs, as it says, "Then the legs of the lame will jump as a deer." Feeling of the hand, as it is said, "Lift ye your hands in holiness." Opening of the mouth, as it says, "Who made a mouth to man?" Talk of the tongue, as it is written (Proverbs), "To man is the array of heart's feelings, but from the Lord is the reply of the tongue."

D, H. Said the Lord, "My word stands forever in Heaven." The word represents the angel of healing, as it is written (Psalms), "He sends his word, and he heals them." Word is the power of prophecy, as it says, "And He put His word in the mouth of Balaam."

Dalit is the initial of the Lord's promise. I say to uplift the poor, as the people are not favorable to the poor, as it says, "The wisdom of the poor is disregarded." But when a poor man prays to me, I do not turn him empty, as it is written (Psalms), "God comforts the ashamed poor." The Holy One looks every moment to the poor, and his words are sweeter to Him than the utterances of others, as it is written (Psalms), "Then the Lord listens to the poor, and makes not ashamed his prisoners," those afflicted people, who are imprisoned by their ailments and disease.

Why does the D face the H? Because he who is poor in this life will be rich in life hereafter, like Israel who is poor here, but will be rich in future life. Again, the heathen who are rich here will be poor yonder in the future life.

Why are the wicked prospering? Because God gives them their reward here for the few good deeds they do. For instance, some wicked do charitable works, not for charity's sake, but for the sake of their name being praised, and so they are rewarded here with wealth.

If a man in Israel, who is born under a favorable planet to live a good, happy life, and acknowledge the Lord with all his heart, is humble in his ways and manners, and does not treat the poor in a haughty way, and does not curse, and gives from his wealth to the poor, and to the rich in the shape of a loan, such a man will eat the fruit in this life while the main stock will remain for him in future life and he will become one of the saints on high.

H, or Hei, is the sacred name of the Holy One, by which he created the world, as it is written (Genesis), "Those are the histories of heaven and earth, when they were created." (The initials of the words "they were created" is H.)

From it you learn that the Almighty had no trouble in creating the universe, as the medium he used was the H, the lightest of all the letters (in pronunciation). All the letters, if they are pronounced, he feels through the various organs, as tongue, lips, teeth, and the letters are accompanied by the unclean saliva, but the H, or "Hei" is pure, as when pronounced, no organ is required to help, and no saliva accompanies it.

All the pronounced names of the Holy One are written with H, and with it heaven, earth, this life and life hereafter, and the messianic time, were sealed by it. The letters by which heaven and earth were sealed are twelve, corresponding to the twelve hours of the day and those of the night, to the twelve months of the year, corresponding to the twelve planets in the Zodiac. To the twelve tribes corresponding to the twelve continents, bearing the twelve names of the twelve tribes, as it is written, "He placed the borders of the nations to the numbers of Israel's tribes." All these letters are as fire, and they glitter as lightning, and each letter measures 21,000 miles, and on each are chained crowns of glory as they are engraved by the finger of the Holy One.

They are also the seals of the Lord, with which he seals all the souls on the glorious chariot. Each name has a special seal. The Lord sits on a throne of fire, surrounded by fire pillars with the sacred names thereon. By each pillar numberless angels of fire are standing. When a man knows those names, and makes use of them, all the heavens are filled with fire, and they go down to burn the earth, but the heavens are linked and chained to the borders of the earth, and seeing the seal of the Holy One, they are filled with the spirit of mercy and do not destroy the earth.

S, or Sain, is the name of the Holy One, as Sain means "maintainer," as the Lord is the maintainer of all.

The Almighty has the key of woman, as it is written, "He opened her womb;" the key of rain, as it is written, "He will open you his best treasure;" the key of maintenance, as it is written, "Thou openest Thy hand to satisfy all with good will;" the key of human structure; the key of manna, as it is written, "He opened the heavens above;" the key of kingdoms; the key of eyes, as it is written, "Then the eyes of the blind will be opened;" the key of the deaf, as it is written, "The ears of the deaf will be opened;" the key of the lips, as it is written, "The Lord will open my lips;" the key of the mouth, as it is written, "And the Lord opened the mouth of the ass;" the key of the tongue; the key of the earth, as it is written, "The earth shall open and flourish salvation;" the key of the prisoners, as it is written, "The Lord makes loose the bound ones;" He has the key of Eden, as it is written, "Opened to me the gates of righteousness;" He has the key of the purgatory, as it is written, "Opened the gates and let enter the pious nations keeping the truth."

Do not read Amonim (Truth) only "Amanim," as for the sake of "Amen," which the wicked say in the purgatory, they are redeemed from it. In the later days the Lord will sit in Eden and explain the laws while all the good ones will sit and the celestial family will be on his right, and sun and moon with all the planets to the left, and the Lord will explain the laws of the new Torah, which will be given through the Messiah. At the end, Zembabel will stand up and say, "Exalted and sanctified shall be the Holy great name." His voice will be heard from one corner of the universe to the other, and all existence will say "Amen." The wicked of Israel and those of the heathen in the purgatory will also say "Amen," and their voices will reach before the Lord. The Lord will inquire for them, and the angels of the service will say that they are the voices of the wicked condemned in the purgatory. At that moment the Lord will show His mercy and hand over to Michael and Gabriel the keys of the purgatory to bring them forth from there.

At that time the two archangels will go and open the forty thousand gates of hell. The hell is 300 miles long, 300 miles broad, 1,000 miles thick, 1,000 deep, and when a wicked man falls into it, he never can get out.

The two archangels at that time will bring those condemned forth, they will be washed and cleansed, their wounds healed, and they will be dressed in pure rays of garment and brought before the glorious throne. When they will be before the Lord, they will fall on their faces, bowing, praising the Holy name. At that moment all will join in the eternal praise of the Lord!

Ch, or Chet, means sin. When the wicked are punished in the purgatory for their sins, they repent and they are forgiven and share the future life with all the pious and good ones, and they sit near the "Schechina" (divine womanhood), as they save their broken hearts with repentance, as it is written (Psalm 34), "God is nigh to the broken hearts," and they are dearer to the Lord than the angels.

The angels are distant from the "Schechina" 36,000 miles, as it is written, "Seraphim stand above him."

"Above" in geometrical calculation is "thirty-six thousand." The Schechina is measured twice thirty-six times ten thousand miles, and the celestial mile is thousands of cubits; a cubit is four span and a fist, and a span measures from one corner of the world to the other. The earth is only one foot long, one foot broad, and one foot high up to the first heaven, and yet, those broken-hearted through repentance are nigh to the Schechina.

But those who are proud, the Lord is far from them. Those who are proud are like idol worshipers, and if a man is like Moses, our master peace with him, and has pride, he will not escape the punishment of the hell.

AN ANCIENT JEWISH PRIMER. 715

F, or Feth. Feth means "lime;" that is, the lime from which all was created, and to which all returns, as it is written, "All was from dust and all returns to dust," and dust is lime. Lime is the limo of the future, from which all the good ones will flourish in parties, as the grass of the field with many garments, whose perfume will fill the whole of the universe, as the perfume of "Eden," as it is written (Psalms xlii), "They will flourish from the city as the grass of the field." The city is Jerusalem, as the Lord will start the resurrection only from Jerusalem, as it is written (Ezechiel), "I will give an ornament in the land of the living." Is there a dead land? It means Palestine, which is called "The land of the living," as her dead will be resurrected first.

What will become of those pious ones who are dead in other lands? But at the day of resurrection the Lord will say to the angels, "Go forth and lift up the surface of the ground, and make tunnels through which to bring the good ones from foreign lands to Jerusalem." The angels will take up the four corners of the globe, and shake the wicked from it, and the good ones will be brought to Jerusalem through tunnels; there the Lord himself will resurrect them.

How will the resurrection take place? The Lord will take a trumpet measuring a thousand cubits, the cubits of the Lord, and will blow so that it will be heard from one corner of the world to the other.

At the first blow the world will be shaken up. At the second blow the ground will be divided. At the third blow the bones will be gathered. At the fourth blow the portions of the bodies will be warmed up. At the fifth blow their skins will be shaped. At the sixth blow the soul will be returned into their respective bodies. At the seventh blow they will stand up alive with their garments on.

J, or Jod, means hand and might. We learn from it that the Lord will give in the later days a might, a foothold to the pious ones, as it is written, "I will give unto them a hand and a good name in my house and my walls."

House means the temple, as it is written, "And my house will be called the worship house of all nations."

Wall means Jerusalem, as it is written, "Upon thy walls, Jerusalem, I appointed watches!"

Jod means also gifts, as the Lord will present gifts to all the pious ones, each one with a cup of life's elixir in order to live forever.

Name means that the Lord will reveal to them the pronounced name by which he has created the heavens and earth, in order that they shall be able to create worlds too. Each pious one will get three hundred and forty worlds as a reward for his good deeds. They will have an everlasting name means the pronounced sacred name, with which future life was created. Praise and exaltation that will be the light of their eyes where at one glance they will be able to see from one part of the world to the other.

Kaf, or K, means the hand of swearing (as by swearing we lift up the hand). It will be a hand clutching of joy at the banquet which God will tender to the righteous at the later days when with each one the "Schechina" will walk, accompanied by tens of thousands of angels, around them pillars of lightning, and the elements will dance before them.

Upon that time the prophet said, "O Lord, uplifted is Thy hand." At that banquet, Isaiah will say "O Lord, uplift Thy hand, let not the wicked see the pleasures of the good ones." The Lord will reply, "No; contrary, let them come, and be ashamed;" then the prophet will say, "No; let them not come, and not see."

The Jewish nationality will be called upon to settle that dispute. Mettatron will bring the Jewish nationality before the Lord. Then she will say, "For what am I called here?" Then the Lord will say, "My dear daughter, I like that the wicked shall come and see the pleasures of the good ones." "Let them come," she will say, "and be ashamed."

At that time the wicked will come at the doors of Eden to look and behold the pleasures of the pious ones. They will see how everyone is clad in garment accordingly, and before each is a table of pearl, and before everyone there is a golden cup mounted with precious stones, while the cup is filled with life elixir, and on the table are arrayed many dishes of delicious food, and before everyone the angels are waiting.

Their faces seem to reflect rays of light as that of the sun, penetrating from one end of the world to the other, while the heavens will open their doors, showering upon them a shower of perfumed dew, and its aroma will fill all the spaces in the universe, and millions of angels, harps in hand, will play and sing, while the sun, moon, and the planets will dance.

When the wicked see those glorious things they will ask why is such an honor and pleasure given to those? And the angels will answer, because they kept the laws. Then the wicked will fall upon their faces praising the Lord, saying, "Hail to the nation, that such is to him; hail to the nation, that the Lord is his God." (Psalms cxliv.)

L, or Lamed, is the initial of "Heart understands knowledge." The heart is a reproduction of man; since man has eyes, so has the heart; man has ears, so has the heart; man has a mouth, so has the heart; man has utterances, so the heart; man roars, so the heart; man cries, so the heart; man walks, so the heart. The heart sees, as it is written (Preacher i), "My heart saw wisdom." The heart hears, as it is written (Kings iii), "A heart to hear to judge." The heart talks, as it is written (Preacher iv), "I spoke with my heart." The heart cries, as it is said (Lamentations), "Their hearts cried unto the Lord." Man is consoled, so the heart; as it is said, "And He consoled them, and spoke with their heart." Man legislates, so the heart; as it is said (Judges viii), "My heart to legislate to Israel." Man roams, so the heart; as it says (Psalms xlv), "My heart roams a good thing." Man rejoices, so the heart; as it is written (Samuel ii), "My heart rejoices in the Lord." Man is clean, so the heart; as it says (Psalms li), "A clean heart, create in me, O Lord." Man mourns, so the heart; as it says (Genesis), "And he mourned in his heart." Man is awakened, so the heart; as it is written (Song of Songs), "I slept, but my heart was awakened." Man inquires, so the heart; as it says (Preacher i), "I turned my heart to inquire." Man is wise, and so the heart; as it is written (Proverbs), "The wise heart takes to good deeds." Man is good, and the heart; as it is written (Proverbs), "A good heart is always jolly."

All that is in man is contained in the heart, and the heart is equal to the two hundred and forty-eight portions of the body. There are twelve actions and qualities distributed to the various instruments of the body.

The brain acts through thought and is the thinking machine. The mouth divides the food, the tongue smooths the ground food, the pipes of the lungs do the breathing, and so on.

But hate, love, envy, dwell only in the heart; therefore it is said, "Do not hate thy brother in thy heart; love thy God with all thy heart." God therefore looks only into the heart; as it is written, "Man sees with the eyes, while God looks into the heart."

M, or Mim. Why pronounced with both letters? Because both are on the height of the glorious throne, where they chain the crowns of light. When the time for sanctification comes, and God does not step down from His height, they approach each other saying, "When will I come to see the face of the Lord?" (Psalms.) When the Lord comes down then all the letters open their mouths with song of praise, the open M says, "Thy kingdom is forever," while the closed M says, "And Thy realm is in all the generations."

At that time the Lord takes all the letters and kisses them, placing two crowns upon each—the one the crown of glory, the other a crown of glory. To the open M He gives two crowns, and to the closed M one of ruling and other of majesty, and places one to His right and the other letter to His left, saying, "My letters, which I engraved with pen of fire, my kingdom is only proclaimed through you."

AN ANCIENT JEWISH PRIMER.

With the open M the Lord is called "King of Kings," while with the closed M He is called "Ruler of Rulers." When the two M's hear it, they open their mouths in song of praise, and all the celestials come, fall, and bow before the Holy One, singing and praising the Almighty.

N, or Nun. Why is the one N straight and the other in a resting attitude? Because with them was the soul of man created, as every soul. Sometimes it rests and sometimes it stands. When she (the soul) is in the body she is resting, and when she is out of the body she is standing.

A king wanted once to enter his palace, which was an unclean place, and he says to his servant, Bring the candle in. So the Lord created man from dust, blood, and gall; therefore He placed in him the soul in order to see what goes on in that dark, unclean place, and the soul is the candle of the Lord (Proverbs xxvi). The soul of man is the candle of the Lord, not that of the animal, as the soul of the latter has rest, while that of the former has no rest.

When man dies, his soul is brought before the celestial bench, and there all the deeds are arrayed, and the judges tell all he did on that day or on that hour and place; even the private conversation between husband and wife is recorded. If he lost his children when he was alive, they ask him, "Why did you lose your children?" If he was blinded, or became deaf in life, they ask him to account for it, as the ways of the Lord are even and only sinners are stumbling on them. They ask him why he stumbled on his sin. If he can give a reasonable answer, they accept it; if not, he is whipped with a whip of fire and he turns into ashes. The ashes are scattered to all four corners of the world, then they are collected by four angels, an angel to each corner, and they put the ashes in the grave, to be there till judgment day.

S, or Samech, means the leaner, and it represents the Lord, who leans the fallen ones, as it is written (Psalms cxlv), "The Lord leans the fallen ones." He leans the heavens as well as the globes of the planets below them. Samech means also the Torah, which is leaned on the prophet, books of the scribes, and on the oral law, as it is witten, "The well which was dug by the princes, by the nobles of the nations." Well means the Torah, as it says, "The well of living water." And the law is always compared to water, as it says, "He who is thirsty, go to the water."

Why are the words of the Torah compared to water? Because as water leaves the highest and comes down, so the Torah likes only him who is humble. "Dug by princes," they are Moses and the seventy elders who explained the laws in seventy languages. "The nobles of the nation," they are the scribes, as David, Solomon, Ezra, who have explained the law to Israel.

E, or Ain, means the eye of the law, which is the eye of all eyes and the wisdom of all wisdom, as it is written (Psalms xix), "The law of the Lord enlightens the eyes." Wisdom is only the wisdom of the law, as it is written, "Ye shall keep my laws, as they are your wisdom and understanding."

P, or Pe, means mouth, and mouth means Moses, as it is written (Exodus), "I am a hard mouth, and a stutterer of tongue." Moses said to the Lord, "I know Thou art the only God, and Thou hast created the world only for Thy own honor, and created man only to do Thee honor, and every portion of the body Thou hast created for some purpose to serve Thee. The head to bow before Thee, the eyes to see Thy glory, the ears to hear Thy honor, the nose to smell, the teeth to grind the food, the pipe to give in and to give out. The veins as blood vessels, the skin for complexion, hands to fight and to work, feet to walk, tongue to talk. Now give me talkative power." The Lord replied, "Who made the mouth and tongue to Adam? Of course I did it."

Z, or Zadic, means the righteous of the world, God Himself, as He does right to every creature in the universe. If God had not given to man mouth and tongue the world could not exist for a moment. When Moses refused to accept the mission on account of being a stutterer the creatures of the world began to tremble, saying, "Behold Moses who once will speak with the Schechina one hundred and seventy-five times face to face and will explain every letter and law in seventy languages, yet he says, 'I am a stutterer;' what shall we say?" For that, that Moses made himself incapable on account of his mouth, the Lord uplifted him, as it is written, "and I was standing between you and the Lord," a position which even Mettatron can not have. For the plea that he pleaded, "I am hard of talk," the Lord speaks of him, "Moses, face to face I speak with him." God has appointed Moses as a treasury over all the creation, as it is said, "Moses, my servant, the faithful in my household."

When Moses reached the department of the future and saw the parties of sages, of the Sansechrin, of the Rabbis, explaining the law in forty-nine ways, and then he saw the college of Rabbi Akibah, who explains three hundred and sixty-five reasons for the laws, he said, "I do not want to be the messenger of the Lord." But the Lord knew the reason of his refusal, so He sent Sagnasel, the Prince of Wisdom, to Moses, and he brought him into the colleges where the laws are taught.

There Moses heard the Rabbis saying "That law, as well as this law, is delivered by Moses from Sinai." As Moses heard this he was calm, and with satisfaction accepted the mission as a redeemer.

K, or Kof, means Moses who surrounded Pharaoh with all words of wisdom in seventy tongues. When Moses and Aaron appeared before the king they found there seventy writers writing the correspondence in seventy languages.

As soon as they beheld the two messengers, how their faces were shining like the sun, and each word they uttered was of fire, and seeing the stick upon which was engraved the pronounced name, they began to tremble, throwing away their pens and letters, bowing in fear before Moses and Aaron.

Then the king asked them, "Who has sent you to me?" They replied, "The God of the Hebrews." He asked again, "What is His name, what of His strength, how many countries has He conquered, how many are the numbers of His fighting army?" They answered him, "His strength is full the universe, Heaven is His throne, His word is fire and shakes up mountains, His bow is fire, His arrows are of fire. He is the creator of all and the peacemaker between fire and water. With His word He created the world, by utterance formed the mountains, and by wisdom He creates the child in the womb of his mother. He clothes the skies with clouds, and lets rain fall upon the earth to maintain the life of all." Said the king to them, "I do not need Him, as I created myself," as it is written (Ezechiel xxviii) "Mine is the Nile and I created me. What you say," the king continued, "that He makes rain and dew; my Nile waters my land to bring forth the sweetest fruit. But wait; I will bring the memoranda of yore, containing the letters of ancient kings; perhaps I will find among them some letters of your God, for, so far as I know, He never has sent to me any writings or greetings." He opened his museum and called upon the seventy writers to read in seventy languages at the same time. Not finding His name, he said to Moses and Aaron, "I know neither of Him nor of His might." He then sent word to all the wise men in Egypt to inquire, and they said, "Yes; we heard about the name of their God; we heard that He is the son of wise, the son of ancient kings." At that time the Lord said, " Fools, ye call yourselves 'wise ones' and me the son of wise, the son of kings," as it is written (Isaiah xiv), "Only fools are the princes of Zoan; the wise counselors of Pharaoh have foolish advice; for how could you say to Pharaoh that I am the son of wise, the son of kings?"

R, or Reish, is the Almighty, who is the head of the world and its end. R is the word of the Lord by which He has created the seven heavens. R is the meaning of head, which means Israel, whom the Lord has made the head of the heathen.

Sh, or Shein, means teeth; those are the teeth of the wicked, which will be broken three times—one time here in this life, second in life hereafter, third in the Messianic time. As the Shein has three heads, so the Almighty will break the teeth of the wicked three times.

The teeth of the wicked will grow out of their mouths 22 cubits long at the time of the Messiah. The people will wonder upon, and they will be informed, that is because they ate up the wealth of the pious in life.

The Shein has three branches, symbolizing the three worlds in which man lives—this life, life hereafter, and the life of the Messianic era. The Shein symbolizes the three sanctifications of this world—the sanctification of the Lord, the sanctification of the Sabbath, and the sanctification of Israel.

T, or Taw, means longing; man longs for everything in this life. Man is born naked, without dress, without shoes, without knowledge, without understanding, without thought, without word, without tongue, without law, without strength, without power, without riches, without wife and children, without walk and deeds; yet as soon as he goes out from his mother's womb he longs only to talk of the tongue, and when he gets it he longs to the walk of the feet, and when he gets it he desires knowledge, and his desire extends gradually to all things he sees. But when he parts from this, he goes out empty, as it is written (Kings ii), "The days of David approached to their end." The day of the king is not written, only of David, as there is no kingdom at the day of death.

Rabbi Aha used to say, "The end of the best is to be killed, the end of man to die, and all are ready for death. Hail to him whose labor was in the law and did the will of his Creator, grew with a good name, and parted from the world with a good name. On such a man is written, A good name is better than good oil, and the day of death better than the birthday."

UNITED STATES BUREAU OF EDUCATION.
CHAPTERS FROM THE REPORT OF THE COMMISSIONER OF EDUCATION

FOR 1894-95.

PROTECTION OF ITALIAN EMIGRANTS IN AMERICA.

EDUCATION AND THE TALMUD.

PUBLICATIONS OF THE BUREAU OF EDUCATION.

SCIENTIFIC TEMPERANCE INSTRUCTION.

WASHINGTON:
GOVERNMENT PRINTING OFFICE.
1896.

CHAPTER XLV.
THE PROTECTION OF ITALIAN EMIGRANTS IN AMERICA.

By LUIGI BODIO.

One of the most important questions treated at the Geographic Congress in Rome, in September last, was that of the care and protection of emigrants. The resolutions adopted at the Geneva Congress of 1892 were (in substance) that colonization laws should include a small plot of land for the emigrant so that he might, as cultivator, be assigned to proprietorship. The Italian Government should have an office of information so as to keep in touch with the colonization going on in foreign countries, as well as with the actual conditions of the colonists; that, in addition to private associations interested in emigration, a public association should act in concurrence with emigration agents, so as to give aid to the emigrant and help him to acquire land; that the emigration laws of 1888 should be modified as regards agents, subagents, guaranties, etc.

The Congress (of Rome?) recommended that the military laws be made less stringent for Italians living in foreign countries, without, however, interfering with the principle of obligatory military service.

Now, it may be stated that, in the last few years, emigration has been diminishing in intensity, not alone from Italy but from all Europe. The Italian emigrants to the United States numbered about 70,000 in 1893 and only 39,000 in 1894. Emigration to Brazil oscillates, too, from year to year, namely, 40,000 Italians in 1887, 104,000 in 1888; 36,000 in the succeeding years; in 1891, 183,000; with a drop to 43,000 in 1894. In the Argentine Republic the Italian immigration was 75,000 in 1888, and 88,000 in 1889; then in successive years 39,000 and 15,511 in 1891, with a later increase to 37,000.

As the social and economic conditions of the countries furnishing the emigrants can not suffer such mutations from year to year, it is evident that those variations depend upon the prosperity and crises in the countries where colonies are established, hence efforts should be made to protect the emigrants from the obstacles which they encounter. Emigration is a necessity for our country [Italy], and we ought to wish that in the present agricultural and industrial conditions, with so little capital to dispose of, thousands more may go forth where they may find work.

The density of population is 107 to the square kilometer in Italy, the average in Germany is 97, in Austria 80, in France 72. France has abundance of capital, land cultivated to the highest degree, conditions of ease and competency in rural districts, and a third less population than in Italy, where the conditions are so different, the poor peasantry and workingmen having become a peril to the social equilibrium. So that emigration becomes an aid to those who are left, as, with the capital in hand, they can more advantageously carry on manufactures and develop agriculture.

Discussions of the colonization of Eritrea (Italian possession in Africa) are very earnest, and the Hon. Franchetti, who has studied the subject on the spot, states that at least 4,000 lire ($772) capital, to be provided by the Government, is requisite for a family of seven persons, in order to construct cabins, to obtain proper implements, to develop their lands, to survey the land, to prepare waterworks, etc.

There is also discussion in regard to colonizing Sardinia and of populating the Campagna (di popolare l'Agro romano), but this, too, requires capital, and there are various obstacles, which, especially on the island of Sardinia, complicate matters. [Here follow laws governing taxation, etc., in Sardinia; objections to home colonization, want of capital for waterworks, and proper sanitation.] But in America our emigrants do not require subsidies from the mother country; they are, to be sure, at a disadvantage the first year, owing in part, to want of organization; but they carry with them a little money, a few tools of trade, and do not leave debts behind.

Our duty is to protect and patronize voluntary emigration—the only form of it which bears with it latent energy, the force of initiative, and the resistence to whatever bars the emigrant's road to success in a new country, or in his native country. Our duty is to aid the masses in procuring employment suited to their condition, to prevent interested agents taking advantage of their good faith, to overcome the obstacles, to seek openings for them, to bring the emigrants into the neighborhood of agricultural and mining sections, dockyards, etc., as may be suited to their previous training or condition in life.

The agents for emigration number 34 in Italy; warranty, 2,690,000 lire ($519,170); subagents, 5,172 in 1892, increased to 7,169 to date. They have more than doubled in some provinces within a few years.

In Switzerland the laws restrict the number of subagents; once there were about 400, paid according to the number of emigrants received, so that there developed a kind of propaganda. A law of 1888, modifying that of 1880, imposed a bond of 3,000 lire ($660) and a tax of 30 lire ($5.79). As a result, the subagents decreased to 170. Swiss laws now prevent propaganda, or enforced emigration, as the consent of the federal council is required before closing a contract with any person having to do with the emigrant, to which person money may be paid for the journey by societies, foreign governments, or private corporations of other countries. Our [Italian] laws do not forbid the emigrants going away if the money has been paid down by government or a colonization society, but if the amount has been exacted from the emigrant the agent is to see that the emigrant receives double that amount. In any case, the regulations are nil which require the emigrant to work his passage either on ship or other means of transport. Some of our emigrants are given free passage by the authorities of Brazil, who desire peasants with families in good, healthy condition and capable of taking hold of some class of work. The governmental arrangements are made with banking firms, who take the responsibility of forwarding the emigrant from a European port to a Brazilian port.

[Signor Bodio then goes on to state the methods employed in Switzerland and in Italy to prevent the taking advantage of emigrants, and the punishment awarded to agents, subagents, etc.]

New laws are being made restricting subagents, getting a better class of educated persons in such positions; forbidding innkeepers, liquor dealers, railroad agents, etc., to be subagents. Experience has taught that interested persons are not proper subagents, if the emigrant is to be dealt justly with. In place of closing the contract just as the emigrant embarks, this is to be done (when the laws go into force) at the point of starting out, so that there may be time to see that all regulations are adhered to. No minors are to be allowed to go as emigrants unless an older person is responsible for them at the beginning and close of the journey. If the committee stationed at a place of embarkation refuse to take the emigrant, the agent is to see that he be returned to his home and his goods with him, and that he receive whatever sum he [the emigrant] may have paid out. To date, the public charities have taken such matter in hand. If the emigrant has reached the foreign land, the agent is responsible for his return, if refused admittance by the authorities, because the laws governing emigration are known to him. If the emigrant finds that he is not being properly treated, he may reclaim his rights from the consul, or from the director of the Italian Aid Society, who is to present such claim to the nearest consular agent. Verbal statements are permissible to consuls, immigrant agents, etc., in the foreign countries, and as a last resort, in case of punishment, the minister of the interior may be appealed to. [These and other regulations are described to prevent the agent tyrannizing over the emigrant.]

As for military regulations: The recruit living in a foreign country submits to the physical examination by a physician before the Italian consul. If received he is sent to Italy, free of expense, on a ship of the Italian Navigation Company. If, for family reasons, health, or study, he desires to go to his country for a three months' period, he can do it with the permission of the consul and of his commandant. The old controversy relative to double nationality should be eliminated in future. The best solution seems to be that which holds between Spain and Argentina. When the person claims to be of one or the other nationality, the matter is to be decided in accordance with the laws where resident. If this seems hardly to agree with the principle jure sanguinis, established by the Italian and other European codes based on Roman law, it is the principle of the nationality jure loci, which—we can not fail to recognize it—is an outcome of the political conditions in the young American States. Thus, if he be born in Argentina of an Italian father, he would be considered an Argentinian as long as he remains in America; should he come to live in Italy he would be considered an Italian.

Now let us see what protection is given to our emigrants arriving in American ports. The minister of foreign affairs, Baron Blanc, has succeeded in obtaining an important concession from the Government of the United States, and has created an office of inspection and protection of Italians at Ellis Island, where emigrants disembark for New York. It is a noticeable fact that even prior to the industrial and commercial crises, a feeling prejudicial to immigration was found among the people, on account of cheap labor, for European workingmen were willing to receive salaries inferior to those of American laborers. Hence American legislation endeavored to limit immigration. The limitation included sick people, paupers, those engaged for contract labor. The majority of those sent back by the Federal immigration agents at Ellis Island are Italians who, poorer than other nationalities, have made contracts to go to work, and state that at once, as they suppose they will be quickly received in America if they are not liable to become objects of charity. Yet they are inexorably repulsed because of the very laws of limitation (contract laws). The American officials frequently turn back our emigrants who have left wife and family in Italy, under the clause of "undesirable immigration," because they [the Italians] make declaration that they have been in America before without naturalizing themselves, and that they do not intend to become citizens; or else it resolves itself into the fact that they have made their money in America and returned to their home, then they come back to the United States again to repeat their former success. The United States welcomes emigrants who may become a permanency and assimilate themselves with the American people, who desire to take part in its political life, learn the language of the country, settle down and have families, the children of which (by aspiration and character) become Americans. But "birds of passage" they do not welcome. It is not so much the quantity as the quality of the immigrant which the United States authorities desire to control, for the nonassimilating elements among emigrants are not in harmony with the social and political conditions of the Republic. In 1894-95 there were 731 Italian emigrants sent back out of 33,902 who reached Ellis Island. The economic condition of our emigrants to the United States is demonstrated by the inquiries made by the American authorities, for the newly arrived individual is asked to show how much money he has. The 33,902 who disembarked at Ellis Island had $362,000, or $10.23 each; included among them were those sent back as paupers and undesirable immigrants. In 1893-94 similar statements hold good. Our minister of foreign affairs interested himself to protect the emigrants in America and to disarm that prejudice toward our compatriots. And this is in fact the basis of the most loyal cooperation, the effort to suppress enforced emigration, either from within or without. In June, 1894, an American office was opened at Ellis Island in connection with the Federal office of immigration, in which office such information could be obtained as is furnished by State boards of immigration, by railroad lines, by corporations and individuals, inducements for work, etc. The Secretary of the Treasury permitted our ambassador to suggest one or more Italian agents for that office who could give the necessary information and make the needed suggestions to our emigrants. Prof. Alex. Oldrini, a young cultured Italian familiar with the United States from a residence there of ten years, was made the first agent, and Chevalier Egisto Rossi, who wrote a work on the United States of America, was made the second agent.

It is to be hoped that the Italian Government will now do its part by furnishing these agents with whatever is requisite, so that they may be able to aid the emigrants in finding occupations, obtaining lands, etc. The Italian Government has, to date, the expenditure of $500 a month for the two commissioners and their office, but the work of these agents ought not to limit itself to assisting the Italian emigrants in connection with the American office, if that office believes it necessary to send them back on account of one or another law, but the Italian agents should be situated to aid the emigrant in obtaining another hearing so that he may disembark and continue his trip to some other State.

It is not enough that our agents aid the emigrants against unfair treatment, on shipboard or shore, but they should be able to give them information concerning the States where they are best able to obtain work, to settle as agriculturists or in mining districts rather than to remain in New York, where their condition is deplorable. Means are lacking so far to bring the Italian agency in New York to this point of efficiency. For it is necessary that the agents be so situated that they can travel to other parts of the States, so as to determine for themselves as regards climatic conditions, the agrarian conditions, violability of contracts, etc. Of the 31,000 Italian emigrants who arrived in the United States in 1894–95 about 20,000 passed the office of our commissioner (Oldrini) direct for New York and its environs, and about 14,000 were forwarded to other States, where they had families, or to mining districts, etc. It is deemed advisable to aid them to go to the Central States, to the mines of Colorado, to Michigan, Minnesota, to Texas ranches, or to the fruit-growing regions of California. A sum of $10,000 is required to place the Italian emigration office in New York upon a suitable footing, to institute a labor bureau, such as is found at the barge office for Germans and Irish, so that the emigrants will not have to deal with the bosses (or padroni), as is now the case, but will find that they can obtain all information at this bureau, or colonization office. With such a sum at disposal, there might be a savings bank, or bank of deposit, arranged with such securities that the emigrants would not again see the bankers disappear with about $150,000 of their savings, as was done one year. Where are we to find the $10,000 requisite for such purpose? In the green book (libro verde) published by the minister of foreign affairs, in which are found the regulations which led to the establishment of the Italian emigration office at Ellis Island, there is a suggestion which seems opportune. It is suggested that 20 lire ($3.86) be required by the Government, from the agency, for each emigrant. As there were in these last years between 33,000 and 65,000 such persons, this amount would be soon acquired. The minister who foresaw the need of protection for the Italian emigrants in the United States also saw the need of such protection in other countries. In Argentina the Italian is as in his own home. In Brazil there is need of such an office of control, for of the Italians going to Brazil it is necessary to distinguish between the State colonies and those of private enterprise. Many Italians are well placed in Brazil, others have to undergo many hardships ere they obtain tolerable positions. The organization of these colonization enterprises needs modifying, for oftentimes the promises held out are not lived up to.

Monopolies, depreciation of money, exorbitant prices, are among the obstacles to contend with. If a few commissioners, or regularly established governmental agents, were connected possibly with the legations in the different countries, they would be useful to the colonists in many cases, and would render abuses impossible, etc. It will be a fortunate day for Italians going to Brazil when authorized agents are there to aid them at embarkation and on their farther trips inland. It is to be hoped that public opinion in Italy will become more favorable to emigration. The outcome of this will be that the proprietor, in order to obtain help, will pay better wages, and emigration will not be synonymous with untold misery at home.

We may look upon emigration as a step in advance toward the bettering and equalizing of conditions. Rather than solicit the return of the emigrant to his native land, rather than regret that emigration transforms itself from temporary to permanent, we should rejoice that the quality of emigration is improved, the arrangements become more stable, the families are reunited, the mother country influence is strengthened.

Emigration is a good thing for the mother country—we utter this sentiment earnestly. It is the safety valve, or security, against envy and class odium, an efficacious instrument in the equalization of human forces. And for Italy, as for all peoples who are late in entering upon new conditions, emigration is a school for the civilizing processes along scientific lines and in adopting new methods. Thus it is the duty of those who have already entered upon the new phases of civilization to assure vigorous protection to the advance guard, composed in part of youthful blood. Protection, material aid, and guidance should be offered to the emigrant. And I salute with great pleasure that part of our emigration which is going to settle in the midst of a people, superior through their methods, perseverance, and economic power, in the very heart of the dominant people of to-day—the Anglo-Saxon race.

This race is the dominating one to-day, because it is educated to a spirit of reform, which opposes the resigning of one's rights, the frittering away of individual energy, opposes apathy toward work, etc.

It is necessary to take the world as it is, and it should be repeated in the chief towns of communes that the emigrant is the best exponent of his country's needs (the best drummer for his own country), and that after him come the experts sent out from the manufactory, the authors, the diplomatists, and lastly the defense by means of the army.

ED 95——57

CHAPTER XLVI.
EDUCATION AND THE TALMUD.[1]

By NAPHTALI HERZ IMBER.

CONTENTS.

Introduction.
Primitive education among the various nations.
The Chaldeans.
The Hebrews.
The Egyptians.
The Greeks.
The Romans.
The Norsemen.
Mosaic educational laws.
Moses in the land of the Chaldeans.
Moses and the Bible.
Moses breaking patriarchal systems and traditions.
Moses hoisted the Chaldean emblem in place of that of Elohim.
Selecting teachers.
Laws to teach.

The school of the prophets.
From the building of the Temple to the exile.
In the school of the captors.
Educational reform by the Great Synod.
The Talmud.
The two Talmuds.
Disfranchisement of the ignorant.
Rabbinical educational laws.
The teacher.
The public schools.
Punishment.
Vacations.
Educational duties of parents.
Religious education.
Babylonian education.
Methods employed in the public schools.
Titles and terms.
From the Great Synod up to the time of Jehoshua ben Gamla.

INTRODUCTION.

When the battle of Koenigrätz was fought, ending with a decisive victory for the Prussians over the Austrians, Prince Bismarck spoke those winged words: "The schoolmaster has conquered." Indeed, that famous battle was an excellent illustration of the great power of education, and the Prussian schoolmaster has shown that his pen could penetrate deeper than the shot and shell of the Austrians. Even the ancients knew of the great influence of education, and Jewish history has recorded a fact which is equal to that of Koenigrätz. "Jerusalem," says the Talmud, "was besieged by the Romans, and the once powerful Hebrew nation was crushed to death by the legions of the pagans. While Vespasian besieged the City of the Lord, wherein civil war and starvation killed more people than the arrows of the Roman archers, an humble Rabbi, Johannes ben Saki by name, knelt before the great victorious Emperor, praying for mercy for his people. 'What shall I grant you?' asked the proud victor. 'Grant me,' replied the sage in a low voice, 'the school of Jahne and its schoolmasters.'" The victor granted the request. He probably never dreamed that from that little school the national spirit of the Hebrews would rise with more vigor. How could he, when it looked as though the whole nation were wiped from the face of the earth. Jerusalem was a pile of débris; her people had been slaughtered by thousands or made cripples. Those

---

[1] An historical sketch of educational evolution among the ancient Hebrews and other primitive nations.

who escaped death were carried into captivity to be made a show of, serving as living trophies for the home-coming victor in his triumphal march. Under such circumstances and conditions the remnant of the Jewish race was found at the time of the destruction, so that even the best patriots could not dream of an attempt at restoration. Yet fifty-five years after the destruction the national spirit which was kept alive in the little school of Jabne arose with vigor, and the 25,000 pupils of Rabbi Akiba, those penmen drilled by the schoolmaster, restored the national pride to its olden glory. The heroic struggle of Bar Kochba (the Son of the Star), who was proclaimed king of the Hebrews, is known to fame, and the coin he used is still preserved in museums as a silent witness of the successful attempt and the vital power of the nation. Now, who performed this marvel, which seemed an impossibility? The schoolmaster from Jabne. The educator blew into the dry, dead bones of Judah the breath of life, and they were resurrected to activity.

Education is not only a power in a struggle, it is also a preserver of life, and the reason for the preservation of the Hebrew race is its wonderful, early developed education. Every Jew, no matter of what standing or reputation—even those from darkest Russia, where 99 per cent of the natives can scarcely sign their names, even those Jews—is able to read and write in his own language. In America we have a vivid picture of the great power of education, for what has made this country so great in every respect, if not the schoolmaster? Instead of being in the rear guard, it is marching onward—a pioneer of culture, leading the advancing march of progress. All this is due to education. The educational system of the United States is its best bond for its continued greatness. The American schoolmaster may reflect, while sitting at the foot of the Washington Monument, upon the educational system of the ancient Hebrews, two thousand years ago, and be interested in the discovery that there is a wonderful parallel between that and his own, of the nineteenth century. To those who observe the march of civilization it will be of great historical value to know the educational system of the Hebrews, whom Mohammed styled "Rigel el Kitab," i. e., "the people of writing."

PRIMITIVE EDUCATION AMONG VARIOUS NATIONS.

I.—THE CHALDEANS.

Among the cultured nations of the ancients the first in rank are the Chaldeans, whom we may style the educators of the world. There was hardly a branch of science wherein they did not prove themselves the masters. In the divine arts—music and painting—they were far ahead of the cultured sons of Hellas. The first symphony was sung by the Chaldeans. The Greeks learned from them when they invaded the country under Alexander the Great. The ancient Jewish notations of music, used by the singers of Zion in the Temple, are all called by their Chaldean names. As a proof of this, it may be stated that the Hebrews learned and adopted the Chaldean musical Alpha Beth, as they adopted from them other useful things pertaining to culture and civilization.

In making or in reproducing pictures they reached the highest standard of perfection at that time. Two prophets give evidence of their skill in that fine and divine art. One described their painted pictures on the walls, engraved with an oily color; the other calls their country "the land of sculptured images, of which they are proud."

In architecture and engineering they surpassed the Egyptians, and the fabulous Tower of Babel was built before the corner stone was laid for any of the pyramids. Jewish legends tell us that they built that tower in order to produce rain by beating the roof with hammers, thus causing the air to vibrate. That is another evidence of their far-advanced science and culture. Their canals and other artificial waterways have long been the admiration of historians.

In astronomy, their fame in that truthful science, which requires a knowledge of mathematics, is still renowned. They were the first to look on high and draw a map

EDUCATION AND THE TALMUD. 1797

of our solar system, dividing the planets in the zodiac. The art of calendaring, for which the ancient Hebrews were renowned—so that in a dispute with Roman astronomers the former claimed that the sun is stationary, while the planets revolve round the fireball (the sun), which argument the latter refused to accept—was learned and adopted from the Chaldeans, as the Jewish names for the months and planets are Chaldean terms, thus telling us plainly in what school the Hebrews had been taught.

In religion they showed themselves far superior to even the Hebrews, as their religion was pure and simple and could not conflict with common sense and feelings. They approached the altars in their houses of worship with silent salutation, and venerating bows, prayers, and music were the offerings, not animal or other kindred sacrifices, as is plainly indicated at the dedication of the great image made by King Nebuchadnezzar on the plain of Dura. Those who understand how to read the Bible between the lines will discover that Jehovah was known to the Chaldeans and worshiped before He revealed himself to Moses in the burning bush, and Nimrod was a mighty hunter before Jehovah; and Jehovah calls the King, Nebuchadnezzar, through the mouthpiece of His prophets, "my servant." It is probable that Abraham, who left Ur of the Chaldees for Palestine, was forced to flee, being persecuted by the Jehovists. (The name Elohim, which means two in one, is mentioned by all the patriarchs until Moses, who restored the ancient Jehovistic cult of the Chaldeans.) The name "Chaldean" means a wise man, and in the Scripture it has the same meaning, where the Chaldeans are termed "the wise men of the East."

Such achievements are impossible without the regular working system of education. Indeed, legend, which is the best informer where history is silent, points in that direction. There is a written Jewish folk story which says that Abraham was when a boy a pupil in the schools of Shem and Eber. Of course there is no historical proof to confirm that legendary statement; still there is a clear passage in the Scripture which indicates some educational progress, when King Nebuchadnezzar orders that children of Hebrews shall be selected, being without physical defect, good-looking, and bright, and taught to write (in the text-book) the language of the Chaldeans. Aside from that record, how is it that the Hebrews, who were in Egypt four hundred years, did not carry away with them a single thought of the land? Not even an Egyptian word, with one exception, is to be found in the whole Scripture, while whole sentences of Chaldean are found. During the stay of seventy years among the Chaldeans the Hebrews seem to have been perfectly nationalized, and the big volumes of the Talmud are treasuries of Chaldean science and literature under the guise of the Hebrew religion. To explain this phenomenon we must think one of two things, either there was a law compelling everybody to read and to write, or the government indirectly offered opportunities even to strangers to be educated, as the enlightened Government of the United States offers educational advantages to all. At all events, there was an educational suffrage, and to it is due the wonderful civilization of the Chaldeans.

The reasons for the early development of education can be given as follows:

1. The nation was not divided into classes and castes (except in the branches of science, as Chartumim, readers of hieroglyphs; Asholim, secret readers; Measphim, magicians; Chasdim, astrologers). The absence of castes prevented education from being monopolized, as in other nations, by a certain class.

2. Their Jehovistic cult with its fatalistic view that the fate of man is written in the stars; hence, if the horoscope told that the child of a beggar would be one day a prophet or a sage, he was brought up accordingly.

3. The simplicity of their quadrat letters with perfected punctuation and vowels enabled everyone to learn writing easily, and it became a common method of exchanging thought. The Hebrews, after their exile, adopted the Alpha Beth of the Chaldeans, with all its grammar and rules. It is a pity that we have no record; but underlying the whole Rabbinical religion the Chaldean cult exists. The only direct proof of the educational power of the Chaldeans is found in their offspring,

the Nestorians. Those Christians, the few living descendants of the Chaldeans, are superior even to the Armenians, not to speak of the wild Kurds among whom they live.

II.—THE HEBREWS.

By the Hebrews I do not mean those Jews who claim to be the children of Abraham, Isaac, and Jacob, for there were Hebrews in the land of Canaan long before Abraham was born. Joseph tells in prison his tale of woe that he was stolen from the land of the Hebrews. As Joseph was the third generation from the first patriarch, who, unlike his son, was not blessed with many offspring, he could not have alluded to the farm where Jacob lived with the few souls of his household, when he spoke of the land of the Hebrews. Even the prophet mentions twice to the Hebrews that their father was an Amorite and their mother a Hittite (while Abraham and Sarah were both Chaldeans). Those Hebrews had another language from Abraham and other customs and religious views from those prevailing in the motherland of the patriarch. When Abraham mingled with those Hebrews he was somewhat undecided, jumping, so to say, from the pure Chaldean monotheistic religion of Jehovah to the dual cult of Elohim which was the original religion of the Hebrews. The confusion of views became in time a matter of grave facts when Abraham became their leader and patriarch. That confusion of views runs like a thread through the whole of Jewish history. The Hebrews, like most of the Semites, had no classes or castes, which is very favorable to educational suffrage; but as they lacked the ability to centralize their national power, like the Chaldeans, they were divided and ruled over by family patriarchs or tribal sheiks. The father of the house was the ruler, endowed with the power of life and death in his home, as the patriarch over the family and as the sheik over the whole tribe. The father was the educator of his son; consequently when the father was an ignorant man the son was obliged to live according to his father's standard, there being no one to educate him. Another stumbling block to education was the birthright and the privilege enjoyed by the firstborn son among the Hebrews. Thus the able-minded children would be neglected for the sake of the weaker minded firstborn son, to whom education might be of no use. In the history of the patriarchs may be found such educational methods with their sad consequences. Often the mother, when she felt a love to one of her children who was of able mind, undertook to educate him, as we read in the history of the early patriarchs. In such a case moral and domestic education were better implanted in the heart of the child, as women are, as a rule, better educators than men. Poor as their methods were, still poorer were the subjects in which they were reared and educated. A fabulous, narrow view of the ruling forces, some duties toward parents, some folklore and tales, formed the whole programme of primitive Hebraic education. In addition, there were the new religious views and customs imported by Abraham from the Chaldeans. He also brought with him the letters of his native land, the plain quadrat Alpha Beth. The patriarch soon acquired the simple language of the Hebrews (the language of the Scripture), but he could not find their writings,[1] which are half hieroglyph and half a zigzag outline. So it came to pass that the minority, who were the offspring of the Chaldean patriarch, were brought up in the easygoing Chaldean writing, while the Hebrews were taught in their old imperfect native Alpha Beth. When the patriarchs migrated to Egypt, taking with them those Hebrews whom they governed, owing to their isolated position in the hermit kingdom the confusion still remained, and education was continued on the same lines until the time of Moses.

III.—THE EGYPTIANS.

The Egyptians had no inborn, natural culture. Hence education was monopolized by the priests, and its blessings, like all other importations, could not be enjoyed by the poorer class. In spite of the 10,000 mummified cats which are claimed by

---

[1] The ancient letters of the Hebrews are still used by the Samaritans and on old Jewish coins.

learned men as evidence of their high civilization, I declare that they were only amateurs in culture. There is a land bordering on Egypt known as Ethiopia, which includes also a part of the famous Soudan. In that land once waved the standard of civilization, and, according to the records preserved in the Talmud as well as from Biblical sources, we can see what a highly cultured people once lived in Darkest Africa. The art of hieroglyphs was imported into the land of the Nilo from Chartum. Hence the hieroglyphs were called Chartumim. That sounds better than the mew of those 10,000 mummified cats and kings, which was a strange culture, not sprung from the people, but only enjoyed by the higher castes of the priests. The variety of classes and castes prevented the education from penetrating into the heart of the people, and prevented the nation at large from cultivating a national unity, which is the only security for a people's strength and prosperity. The son of a priest was destined to be a priest, no matter whether his mind could comprehend the mystery symbols of the hieroglyphs or not. The child of the soldier was forced to do the fighting all his life from generation to generation. The offspring of the workingmen were by law required to live their time in the line of work, each according to his guild and union, following in the footsteps of their departed sires. Even the thieves formed a class, a registered caste, and their children had no choice but to live up to the profession of their fathers. Under such a caste system true education was unknown, and the few hieroglyphists had their little knowledge inherited with their cats and rites, it being a handing down from father to son. Again, geniuses, if they happened to be born of parents who were not priests, were condemned to live as ignorant and undeveloped beings. No wonder the Egyptians were in their time the target of jesters and mockers. No wonder that the Hebrews, in spite of their staying there for four centuries, could not absorb a single habit or thought from them. No wonder that there was not a national union, as each caste was a stranger to every other, as black is to white. No wonder that we dig out so many mummified cats, the only inheritance left to the world of an uneducated people.

IV.—THE GREEKS.

The Greeks possessed a national culture with an original civilization framed with the progressive thoughts of other nations. Their religion was that of a smiling, idealistic beauty, answering the sensual emotions, and rousing the sentimental feelings to the highest pitch of inspiration. But, with all the advantages of good government and an inspiring literature, they lacked the best medium which would have made them everlasting, and that was education.

They had an Aristotle, but not a schoolboy. They had philosophical schools, but not a system of education. Plato, in making the plan for his idealistic republic, had it in his mind to place the education in the hands of the government. He was the only philosopher who felt the real need of his people, and that was the want of an education.

Sparta tried to establish an educational system under the care of its republic, but it did not amount to anything, as the sole aim was to train and drill up a republic of soldiers. The consequences of the lack of education were fatal for Hellas. Besides the everlasting fighting among themselves, which has passed into a proverb, "When Greeks joined Greeks, then was the tug of war," they could not maintain their independence, and fell a prey to mighty Rome, then the mistress of the world. What has the Greek culture, so much talked of, left behind it? Nothing except a few busts of shapeless Venuses and the fame of only seven wise men, who bear witness that the whole nation, with its multitudes, remained in darkness so many centuries.

The speculative philosophy of Aristotle is not worth anything, compared to the scientific facts brought to light by the Chaldeans. The sons of Hellas, whose religion, for the sake of its charm, was adopted by other nations, exchanged the gaiety of that old religion for the more meditative one of Christianity, whose worship consists in prayer and fasting, not in the enjoyment of the wine cup and sensual satisfaction—a religion which even the reasoning Romans resisted so long. How can we explain these phenomena? Paul took them by surprise. They were taken in, not by the grand Apostle, the miracle worker, but by the Jewish boy who, as a child, was compelled to visit the public school, then as a youth sat in the college at the feet of the Rabbi Gamaliel, and the Olympian gods and goddesses fell before Paul, the educated.

V.—THE ROMANS.

The reasoning Romans had no talent whatever for producing anything original. Their religion, cult, customs, and manners were all borrowed, adopted, or absorbed from other nations. They were born prize fighters, yet they had one good quality, a love of system and order, a quality which makes the educator. Indeed, there were more Greek mentors in Rome than teachers in Athens. There were fewer ignorant soldiers in Cæsar's legion than in Alexander's famous phalanx. To be a Roman and free was sufficient to gain the privilege of expanding all one's aspirations and ambitions, no matter who he might be. But as Rome was always busy in maintaining her possessions in all the four corners of the world, she cared more about bringing up her children in the arena than in the school, and the educational department was a private undertaking. Still, there was some sort of an education, and under Christianity Rome became the real educator of the world. Italy's schools and colleges in the beginning of the Middle Ages were renowned all over the world.

VI.—THE NORSEMEN.

Along both sides of the straits of the Baltic there once lived a people known as the Norsemen. That great Teutonic race was the only one which became the tutor of Europe, demonstrating the power of education. In character they were knights of chivalry; in valor they had no equals; their tribes routed the Romans by land under the leadership of Hermann, while their kinsmenn, the Danes, raided the isles of the Britons, the mighty fortress of the Romans. The Danes were a seafaring people and ruled the waves from ocean to ocean, and long before Columbus discovered this blessed country the Norsemen had been here to place their advance posts.

Their religion was in some respect the same as that of the Greeks, but had a more serious aspect. Their Odin (the same as in Hebrew and Chaldean Adon, which means the Lord) was not of the brutal character of a Jupiter, who killed his own children. Odin was, as Carlyle says, a man, a leader, a teacher, who invented the Runes, the Scandinavian Alpha Beth. Their Valkyrs were not demoralized demigoddesses, like Venus, but were brave maidens with a spear in one hand and the shield of morality in the other. Their Gambrinus was not a riotous character like the Bacchus of the Greek; he was a social and amiable person—a trait still visible in the offspring of the Norsemen when they gather round the cup. Runes were not, like the writings of other nations, imitations or a modified Alpha Beth, after the model of the Phœnicians, but were the letters of their Alpha Beth bearing the stamp of native self-culture. Odin, the teacher and inventor of those Runes appeared in his rôle among the Norsemen 70 B. C. The simplicity of the Runes, in form, and the ethics of the Norse lore as embodied in the Edda, the Scandinavian Scripture, leads one to suspect that the great Odin was a Chaldean, cast away on the shores of Scandinavia to become the educator of that noble race.

No written records have been preserved to tell of their educational work, but there are left living samples, and by the deeds of the offspring from the Norsemen we can see the consequences of their educative ability.

As Odin was the inventor of the Runes, which were the best medium of education, so, according to the Norse lore, he also invented poetry. Indeed the legend only foreshadows who were the people following in Odin's footsteps as educators. These were, among the Scandinavians, the Scalds; among the Germans, the Bards, the Minnesingers, whose sweet melodies reechoed throughout the great German Empire.

Those poet-singers have with their songs educated in a delightful manner the children of the mighty in their castles as well as those of the peasants. Through such mediums—poetry and those singers—the knowledge required was distributed to all alike. That was the way of education among the noble Norsemen whom some historians delight to style ignorant barbarians. Fortunately, divine Providence has preserved their deeds, through which we may come to know them better.

MOSAIC EDUCATIONAL LAWS.

I.—MOSES IN THE LAND OF THE CHALDEANS.

The Bible may describe the Hegira of Moses and make him shelter himself under the roof of a noble priest of Midian, a short distance from Egypt; a legend of the Jewish folklore may place him in the land of Cush, in Abyssinia, as a king ruling there forty years, marked by a peculiar love affair with a dark-brown princess; still, we, by virtue of his deeds, his knowledge, and assisted by some hints of Rabbinical tradition, are of the opinion that his forty years of exile were spent among the Chaldeans, and a man is better known by his deeds than by his fame or name. We will group and array our witnesses. They are:
1. His religious views.
2. His geographical knowledge.
3. His educational laws.
4. His peculiar laws concerning women.

First, then, in regard to his religious views: Mosaic Jehovah v. Hebraic Elohim.

When Moses appeared as a redeemer among the Hebrews, in Egypt, the Elohistic party was mostly composed of those native Hebrews who followed the patriarch into bondage from their native land of Canaan. The other was the Jehovistic party, who clung to the Chaldean religious opinions, as imported by the Chaldean patriarch, Abraham. It was not exactly that the direct descendants of the patriarch were Jehovistic or the descendants of the others Elohistic, the confusion of their religious views made a party issue not dependent upon the lineage by genealogy. The Elohists were in the majority, hence the great opposition which Moses met with when he first made his appearance among them. When he first proclaimed the name of Jehovah they were so ignorant of it as to doubt his mission, for they had a tradition that Elohim would remember them.

Moses's geographical knowledge, which could accurately outline every hill, mountain, and stream extending from the border of that country where he intended to establish his great Hebrew Empire to the Euphrates, could not have been acquired by studying a map, which was not at that time in existence, but only by traveling through the places he described. His hostility to the patriarchal institutions, and breaking up of the family and tribal sovereignty, placing the power in a central concentrated force, goes to show that he must have known the Chaldeans' ways and their belief in a centralized government.

His disfranchising of women and excluding them from public as well as from domestic rights was another blow to the Elohists, who looked upon the weaker sex as superior beings, the patriarch having been told by Elohim himself to do anything which Sara should say.

The attitude of Moses toward women was the same as the attitude of the Chaldeans toward them. Moreover, the Rabbinical traditions hint plainly that Moses knew or was in the land of the Chaldeans. The book of Job is accredited to Moses as the author, and that he wrote it purposely in Egypt to show the great confidence of the afflicted man in God and how by faith he was rewarded. The simple, yet poetical style and expression of the book, the manifestation of foreign, scientific views, combined with a local knowledge of Egypt, reveal the author and show it to be one of the scriptures of Moses. Looking upon the book, we must say that it is only a propaganda, advocating the Jehovistic religion and praise of the astronomical knowledge for which the Chaldeans were famous. His idea was to demonstrate and illustrate the faith in Jehovah, not in Elohim. For that reason the author created a dramatic person, Job by name, whose wealth was plundered by the Chaldeans (the mention of the Chaldeans is suspicious). The scene in heaven, where Elohim gives a reception to the sons of Elohim, and entertains with them Satan (a person never mentioned in Jehovistic prophets), looks somewhat like a satire on the Elohistic cult. The chapters from the first to the thirty-eighth deal with Job's terrible affliction, and the more terrible consolations, by dispute and argument, of his friends, and during the whole controversy, of a speculative philosophical character, the names of Elohim or Shadai are not mentioned. Failing by their waste of words to help to console or to convince that poor afflicted Job, they seem to retire to where they came from, and from the thirty-eighth chapter to the end Jehovah has the floor and from the midst of a storm he argues with Job, not with poetical words and a speculative "perhaps," but with plain words and plainer facts, based on the phenomena of the solar system and its planetary wonders (such astronomy as was taught by the Chaldeans). Job was, through such facts and array of natural phenomena, converted, convinced of the power of Jehovah and he became a Jehovist, and, through his conversion Jehovah again restored to him his health and wealth. This is an outline of the drama of poor Job, and it seems to have been written in a missionary style for the purpose of converting the readers to the Jehovistic cult, and its author could not have been any other than Moses.

Having established in a general outline the relation of Moses to the Chaldeans, we shall give a detailed account of his educational works, which will make that relation more distinct.

II.—MOSES AND THE BIBLE.

Those who think of Moses as a founder of religion, and his Bible as a religious book, do not fully comprehend the matter. Moses is still called by the Jews "Moshe Rabbina," a term which means, Moses, our teacher. The Bible has no claim to being a religious book, so far as we understand religion to be that religious touch which links us to Infinity, as by prayer, and the belief in the immortality of the soul is not to be found in the whole Scriptures. Nay, more; among the 613 laws there is not one regarding prayer, that foundation of religion. On the contrary, Moses, differing from others, forbade them to build any place of worship except the one place which Jehovah should select. (As among the Chaldeans, whose policy of centralization led them to have only the temple at Babel.) The Bible is an educational code, and its history is the history of education. In order to understand the Scriptures better let the actions of Moses's educational work serve as a commentator.

III.—MOSES BREAKING PATRIARCHAL SYSTEMS AND TRADITIONS.

Moses found the patriarchal traditions relating to the creation and to the deluge in the Elohistic style, ascribing all the events to Elohim. Not being able to root those legends out of the minds of the Hebrews, which seemed to be in their blood, he made additions of other versions with a Chaldean color.

To the first chapter of Genesis, where it mentions how Elohim created a couple, he added another chapter of creation how Jehovah created man from dust and his wife from his rib. In the patriarchal Elohistic version woman's equality with man is plainly indicated, while in the monotheistic Jehovistic narrative the degradation of woman is shown.

In the first chapter of the deluge Elohim requests Noah to bring into the Ark of every creature a pair, without distinction of clean and unclean, while in the Mosaic version Jehovah tells him to bring in from the clean animals 7 pairs, and from the unclean 1 pair. In legislating that man shall forsake his father and mother to cling to his wife he broke and removed the power of parents and patriarchal government, by that law placing the sacred personal liberty above obedience. The only concession he made to the Hebrews was in respect to the firstborn, whom, however, he soon deprived of their rights.

EDUCATION AND THE TALMUD.

IV.—MOSES HOISTED THE CHALDEAN EMBLEM INSTEAD OF THAT OF ELOHIM, AND REMOVED THE HEBREW ALPHA BETH, REPLACING IT BY THAT OF THE CHALDEANS.

When the prophet speaks of Elohim, mentioning his angels, he describes the latter with calf's legs (see Ezek., chap. 1). The Apocrypha tells of Bel in Babel, that he was a monster serpent. The calf was the emblem of Elohim, the serpent was the emblem of Jehovah. When the Hebrews made a golden calf, they simply hoisted the Elohistic emblem, their request to Aaron being, "Make us an Elohim." When Moses came down he destroyed the calf, killed the rebels, and hoisted Jehovah's emblem, the serpent, on high, requiring the Hebrews to look upon that. As the body of the firstborn ones played a great rôle in the Elohistic plot he broke their power entirely, placing it in the hands of a selected body of teachers, the priests and the Levites. Another step in educational reform was taken when he removed the old Hebraic Phœnician Alpha Beth, with its zigzag letters, and replaced it by the simple, readable Chaldean Alpha Beth, with its plain quadrat letters.

The Talmud says Moses gave the ten commandments with an Egyptian word (Anohi, I am) with Chaldean letters, and in the Hebrew tongue. That Chaldean style of writing was a great educational medium for diffusing the knowledge to all.

V.—SELECTING TEACHERS.

In appointing judges Moses did away with the patriarchal power, centralizing it in the hands of the law. He employed the same method in education, selecting a special body of teachers, the priests and the Levites, whose aim should be to teach. As he says, "They, those of the tribe of Levi, shall teach thy laws to Jacob and the knowledge to Israel." In order that they might be devoted to their profession, he did not allow them by the law to have any earthly possessions, such as houses and lands. As they were the teachers of the people their income was from the people in the shape of the tithe from the land and from the flocks. Moses, like the Chaldeans, thought that women were emotional and unfit for teaching serious subjects of a scientific character. They were good for telling tales and stories, but not for higher practical teachings, hence he prohibited a woman from even practicing witchcraft under penalty of death. (Such was also the Chaldean law.) As the primitive science was based upon observation and practice, and as there was a demand for teachers more than for pupils, he gave them such a law—to study science. He gave them laws concerning what to eat and what not, in order to have an opportunity to study natural history. The laws of clean and unclean leprosy and other diseases forced them to study medicine and anatomy. The laws concerning the mixed plantation brought them to learn botany. But the most practical subject of study was the laws governing the calendar and the regulation of the festivals, which were regulated on the astronomical plan of the Chaldeans, even to the division of the weeks, days, and months. By such laws the teachers were educated in the branches of science, and were bound to teach the knowledge thus obtained to their pupils at large. From this standpoint the Bible is the educational code of teachers, outlining the subjects to be taught.

VI.—LAWS TO TEACH.

One of the 613 laws is a special law to teach the children. The law in question is as follows:

"Ye shall teach these laws to your children, they shall speak of them always."

Maimonides declares that in that law is included the law to teach in the sacred tongue. Another law in that line says: "That once in seven years to gather all the people, even women and children, in order that they shall hear and learn." That law is rather to indicate the necessity for religious instruction. "Tell and teach your children," is an obligatory law. It was told to the individual, the father as well as to the nation at large, so that in case there were no parents, the nation took the parental responsibility of educating the children. Instead of the old patriarchal folklore and tales, Moses legislated on subjects to be taught, one history, the other geography, as is to be seen plainly in his request to "Remember the days of yore, to mark the years of generation (history), to ask thy father to tell you; thy elders to explain how the Most High has settled the nations, dividing the sons of man in fixing the borders of nations (geography)." That was the corner stone which the great educator, Moses, laid to his educational structure. How it has grown by other educational architects we will see in the run of history.

THE SCHOOL OF THE PROPHETS.

As soon as the Hebrews invaded Canaan, after the death of Moses, the Elohists by virtue of their majority assimilated themselves with the native Hebrews, whose language they understood and spoke. The consequence of that assimilation was the establishment of the old patriarchal government and the rule of tribal sheiks, as in the days of yore. From an educational standpoint it was the worst period in Jewish history. The adoption of the native Phœnician Alpha Beth made it difficult to study, and the establishment of the Elohistic cult brought in its train the old patriarchal system of government with its endless feuds and tribal wars. The women again came to the front and the educational office was again in their hands, rearing their children on the old system in the oral traditional songs and folklore. No wonder that during the time of the Judges women, as Deborah, Jael, and others, were better educated than the sons of Israel.

The history of education since the invasion of Canaan begins with the seer Samuel, who was the founder of the famous School of the Prophets and the restorer of the Mosaic Jehovistic religion. Samuel made a step of great reform in placing the education in the hands of good, trained teachers not belonging to the Elohistic ignorant sect of priests, as the children of Eli were. The consequence of the restoration of the Jehovistic religion was the centralization in the hands of an absolute king. As the first king, Saul proved unsatisfactory, he was replaced by David. The School of the Prophets was in existence during the four hundred years till the first destruction. The pupils were called "Beni Haubijm" (Children of the Prophets). The prominent masters of that school were: Samuel, Gad, Nathan, Edow, Achyohu from Shilo, Elijah, Elisha, Jehu ben Chanani, Ebadjah, Michah ben Jimla.

That class of prophets was not the same as the authors of Scripture. The former were prophets by virtue of their training and study, while the latter were geniuses inspired by those hidden forces of nature—the marks of the genius of every age. The former distinguished themselves by deeds, the latter by words and orations. The former were strict, stern Jehovists, while among the latter some had an Elohistic leaning (as Ezekiel and others). The School of the Prophets was not stationary. It was always on the move from place to place as this was the only way of distributing knowledge among the classes. It reminds one of the methods of the Scalds, the disciples of Odin. It is curious to note that the first founder of that school, Samuel, was called "Roe," a term which means the seer in the clouds, while Gad and Edow were called "Chosim," which means stargazers. It seems that in progress of time some of the masters had established colleges, as the name of Edow's College, "Midrash Edow," in whose archives were chronicled the events and history of the reigning kings. The result of that educational department could best be seen in the fact that when King David reorganized the caste of the priests and Levites he appointed, under the direction of Heiman, 288 teachers of music. In spite of that, the gates of education were still blocked to the people by the heiroglyphic Phœnician Alpha Beth, which was without vowels and punctuation. The Talmud tells us that when Joab, the commander in chief to David, was ordered to make war on Amalek with the instruction to kill and to wipe out all the remembrance (Seicher) of Amalek as the law says, he went and killed only the males. When questioned about it he replied that his teacher taught him to wipe out the males (Sachor). Such a misreading and misunderstanding was due to the Phœnician Alpha Beth, which had

EDUCATION AND THE TALMUD.

neither vowels nor punctuation. This shows what an important rôle the simple quadrat Alpha Beth of the Chaldeans played in the education of the Hebrews.

I.—FROM THE BUILDING OF THE TEMPLE TO THE EXILE.

The building of the Temple and the reorganization of the priesthood as teachers, which promised to develop education, was also only a promise and of short duration. For no sooner had King Solomon closed his eyes than the unruly party of the Elohists rose as one man, and the ten tribes under the leadership of Jeroboam hoisted Elohim's emblem—that of the Golden Calf. That the separation was from a purely Elohistic point of view we can see by the party issue of its platform, as proclaimed by Jeroboam: "To thy tents, O Israel," which means a restoration of home rule, placing the right over life and death in the hands of parents and tribal sheiks. In spite of the fact that the Elohistic government tolerated to a certain extent the Jehovistic School of the Prophets, the outlook for education was a gloomy one, as it was tempered indirectly by the prophets and priests of Baal. The educational development among the other two tribes who still maintained a Jehovistic sham religion was at a standstill, and during the four hundred years of the Temple's existence the priests were renowned for their blessed ignorance. During that long, sad period of four dark centuries we find only one Jehovistic king, Jehosaphat, who tried to reorganize the priests and Levites, as teachers, as Moses founded them. He, that king, says the Chronicle, sent out the priests and Levites among the people, and with them the book of the written laws of Jehovah, to visit all the cities in Judah to teach among the people. A deplorable case of ignorance can be illustrated: When the High Priest Chilkijah found an old book of Moses in the Temple he could not read it, and gave it to Shapan, the scribe, who, by advice of the King Joshijahn, brought it to the Prophetess Childa for interpretation. It is probable that it was one of the ancient early books of the law, which was written in simple, plain letters with regular vowels and punctuation in the Chaldean Alpha Beth, hence neither the high priest nor the scribe could read it.

To sum up the history of the Jews during the first four hundred years from the building of the Temple to its destruction, we will find that education was better developed under the Jehovistic religion than under the patriarchal system of the Elohistic cult. No wonder that the great Jehovistic prophet, Jeremiah, advocated the invasion of the Chaldeans, who were Jehovists, and he called their King Nebuchadnezzar the servant of Jehovah. The reason for this was that even the last two tribes had come to be worshipers of Elohim. (It is now understood why Nebuchadnezzar favored the author of the Lamentation.) Even the Talmud says "The Almighty did a charitable work in exiling the Hebrews into the land of the enlightened Chaldeans."

II.—IN THE SCHOOL OF THE CAPTORS.

Dr. Karpeles, the present famous Jewish historian, is surprised that the Jews, who were ignorant heathens when they were led into captivity, came out as learned sages after a short stay there. This need not be surprising, as it is probable that they were compelled to be educated by their captors, or were so impressed with the educational institutions of the country that they were indirectly forced to adopt them, as the square Aramic Chaldean Alpha Beth was the best medium for reaching them.

From tablets preserved at the British Museum, to which my attention was called by Dr. Cyrus Adler, of the Smithsonian Institution, we gather that the Chaldeans had, to a certain extent, a regular system of education, assuming the form of educational suffrage. There is a tablet which may be called the exercise or lesson of some Babylonian lad in the age of Nebuchadnezzar. It consists of a list of the kings belonging to the early dynasties, which he had to learn by heart. The fragment of an old primitive folkstory which once formed a part of the First Reader of a lesson book for the nursery shows that the teaching of the child began at the age of 6. The story therein is this: A foundling was picked up in the streets and taken from the mouths of the dogs and ravens, to be adopted by the king as his own son.

The vast libraries for which Babylon was famous were open to the public, and were placed in the temples by order of the king, which shows that the Chaldeans were educated under the control of the government. As a proof of educational suffrage might be mentioned the fact that one of the librarians was the son of "an irrigator," a child of an unskilled laborer. This is a proof of how and to what extent education was spread among the Chaldeans. No wonder that the Hebrews became enlightened in the land of their captors, which was their school. The Talmud says that the Jews brought from Babylon the names of the angels, as well as the names of the months. By the former we understand the religious views, while by the latter they meant the astronomical science of the calendar. In addition, they adopted the Aramic Chaldean Alpha Beth, with its square letters, and probably had nationalized the educational system of the Chaldeans with many modifications according to the demands of the times and circumstances.

EDUCATIONAL REFORM BY THE GREAT SYNOD, UNDER EZRA THE SCRIBE.

Ezra the Scribe, or, as he is called by the Persian King Artaxerxes, "the Scribe of the Law," at the return from the exile, called a congress of restoration, known as "The Great Synod." This body was composed of 120 members, among them prominent prophets, such as Malachi, Chagi, and Zecharje. The object was to show to the people at large how the chain of tradition was unbroken from Moses to the elders, from the elders to the prophets, and from the prophets to the great synod. Ezra's aim in calling that famous congress was to promote a universal education, as the book says of him, "Ezra has prepared his heart to explain the law of Jehovah and to teach in Israel law and justice."

The first thing that body did was to revise the Bible in accordance with the Jehovistic tradition, and many a book has experienced alteration, while some were excluded from the canon entirely.

The next step was of great educational importance, namely, the adoption of the Chaldean Alpha Beth, and the addition of the five letters, m, n, z, p, ch, which were written at the end of words. The restoration of the Chaldeans' well-regulated and easily read Alpha Beth was of far-reaching benefit to educational development among the people, so that the Talmud glorifies Ezra, making him equal with Moses, being worthy that the law should have been given through him. The grateful Talmud also acknowledges the merit of the great synod, in saying that they restored the crown to its ancient glory. It weaves a sacred garland of tradition around the art of writing, declaring that the art of writing and that of engraving were created on the last day of creation, on the Friday at twilight, thus giving an air of divinity to these sciences, uplifting them to the highest standard of spirituality, and making them the distinguishing mark between the divine man and the lower human being.

By declaring human authority superior to the law they have removed the dead letter, which was a stumbling-block to progress, and enabled the living authorities to act according to the requirements of time and circumstances.

By revising the Bible, declaring only twenty-four books of early inspiration, and shutting out the rest from the canon as "outside books" (apocrypha), they opened the gates of knowledge to everyone, since only scientific skill was required, and not prophetic miracles.

By breaking the power of the priestly caste, in taking out of their hands the judicial as well as the educational offices, they gave an opportunity to every citizen to strive for these places.

The proclamation of the oral law as the real esoteric meaning of the written law—as they said that "eye for eye, tooth for tooth," of the Mosaic law means money fines—has made man more divine and God more humane.

The appointment of a supreme court of 71 members, qualified for that exalted

EDUCATION AND THE TALMUD. 1807

position only by knowledge, regardless of birth or family disgrace, did away with the patriarchal system of government and the right of might. Nay, more, the members of the supreme court, who had jurisdiction over the whole nation, who were known as the "Sanhedrim," were required to have as qualification the universal knowledge, not only of the Jewish jurisprudence, but also the most living languages and their literatures, so that the whole body, as one man, should know the seventy tongues spoken at that time by the human race. Even an understanding of the black art, or magic, was required of the member of the Sanhedrin. The declaration that a sage is mightier than a prophet, and that by the power of wisdom the Almighty created the world, gave a value to universal knowledge superior to that of the written law of Moses.

With the exception of the Samaritans, whom they fought to the knife, all nations, without distinction of creed or religion, were invited to eat from the tree of knowledge—to be as the gods.

They declared, in the Talmud, that even a heathen, if he studies the law, is higher than a high priest who goes into the Holy of Holies. In another place they say that a bastard a sage is superior to the high priest. Such declarations show that the charitable desire was to extend the blessings of knowledge and education even to non-Israelites. Indeed, the various disputes about religious and scientific topics recorded in the Talmud between learned Jews and Romans, Persians, Chaldeans, and Greeks, where the latter displayed a knowledge of Jewish literature equal to the rabbis, show that they must have accumulated that knowledge through the hospitality of the Jews, by whom it was regarded as a law that they should extend education to everyone. Through such a broad view of education an avenue was opened by which even the pagans could enter the sanctuary, regardless of lineage.

The following may be cited as an illustration, taken from the Talmud: "It was a custom, when the high priest on Atonement Day left the sanctuary unhurt, for the people to give him an ovation as a congratulation upon his coming out safely. Once, while the people were cheering the high priest, the two noted Shmayo and Abtalyon, who were in direct succession to the great synod in the eighth generation, happened to pass by. The former was the Nasi (spiritual prince), the latter Ab Beth Din (president of the Sanhedrim). The crowd, beholding them, left the high priest and followed the sages, cheering them, who were the children of converted heathens. The high priest felt humiliated, and when he met the sages he saluted them, saying, 'Let the sons of heathens come to peace,' alluding to their lineage. They replied satirically, 'Let the sons of heathens come to peace who do the work of Aaron, and let not the sons of Aaron come to peace who do not do his deeds.'" This is the best illustration of what an exalted position education had given them, regardless of their lineage.

The great reform work of that famous congress, which lasted in continuous session for many years, was solely devoted to education, and every work, no matter of what character, had an educational bearing.

The municipal government was taken from the hands of the Elders and placed in the hands of the "Seven Best Men of the Town," elected by the people. These men were under the control of the Ab Beth Din, the head of the city court, whose special duty, besides executing justice, was to care for the educational department of the town. (Such a court in an ordinary town consisted of three members, while in the capitals of the provinces the body consisted of twenty-three members with the power of passing the death sentence.)

The Temple, which, at the time of the exile, had had the appearance of a huge animal slaughterhouse, was rebuilt and made the center of the federal government with various departments, of which one was a department of education, caring for the maintenance of the higher colleges as well as the public schools for the children in Jerusalem. The Temple was placed under the control of a nonpriest, who had the title of "Ish Habaith" (the lord of the mansion—"major-domo"), who, in turn, was under the control of the Sanhedrim. The high priest, seven days before the Atonement Day, was handed over to two sages, nonpriests, pupils of Moses (which means Jehovists), selected by the Sanhedrim to be trained and drilled for the religious performance. The priests who were instituted by Moses as healers, by the decree of the great synod, ceased to be such. The reason for this was that the priests were not allowed by the law to come into contact with a corpse, and as the science of healing is based upon the knowledge of anatomy, which the priest could not study, that science was cultivated in the colleges by nonpriests, and when graduated, they were recognized as Rofim (healers). From these Rofim one was selected as the "Healer of the Temple," whose duties were the same as those of the modern board of health. The lepers, or other people suffering from skin diseases, who, in former days were cast off from the camp, and were not allowed to join in the Easter feast, being declared by the priests unclean, after the progress of science, says the Talmud, went a day before Easter to the surgeon, who made an operation on them, removing certain worms from under the discoloration, and they were then declared clean and allowed to join in the Easter celebration. By ordering certain prayers and benedictions, the great synod denounced, indirectly, the mode of worship by sacrifice. The famous Lord's Prayer is to be found in the Talmud, with a slight alteration, bearing the air of antiquity. By means of prayers, the great synod gave the Jews that which Moses lacked—a religious education. The decree to build in every habitable place a Beth Hadneseth (a house of worship) and a Beth Hamidrash (college and public library) was of great educational importance. The former gave an idea of Him who is everywhere present, and not only in the Temple; the latter increased the desire for reading. The Talmud says that the great synod fasted twenty-four days, praying that school-teachers and book writers and authors should never accumulate wealth from their profession so that they would be bound by circumstances to live up to a high standard. National congresses for educational purposes were convened ten times in ten different places after the great synod, adding reforms according to time and place. After the great synod there follows an unbroken line of couples or pairs, as registered in the book, The Sayings of the Sires. The bearer of the first name was always the Nasi (the Prince) while his companion was Ab Beth Din (president of the court or Sanhedrim). Rabbi Gamaliel, at whose feet the great Apostle Paul sat as a pupil, was one of the last couples.

The work of the great synod is preserved in the gnomic sayings which they left, in the "Sayings of the Sires," "Be patient in judgment," "Bring forth many pupils and make a fence to the law." Upon that saying, the grand, towering structure of the Talmud was built.

THE TALMUD.

The Talmud, that great written museum containing untold treasures of a civilized world of six bygone centuries, that wonderful and universal encyclopedia, which, with the Mishna and Midrash, which follow in its train, presents twice as many volumes as the Encyclopædia Britannica, that wonderful book, which Orthodox Judaism considers so sacred, written by the inspiration of the Holy Ghost, is not the work of a few individuals, but a work of great scientific importance. It is a work by the whole Jewish nation, as well as by others who indirectly contributed to that remarkable gazette of the world.

The great synod laid the first corner stone to that unparalleled structure, and it was finished a short time before the Hegira of Mohammed. Its various editors in chief, as Rabbi Johannes (who was the first editor of the Jerusalem Talmud), Rabbi Akiba, Rabbi Jehuda, Hanasi (the Prince), who was the editor of the Mishna, were great historians as well as famous scientists. Its contributors were recruited from all the rank and file of society. You will find a contribution from a plain, modest, unskilled laborer, who made his livelihood as a burden carrier, next to an essay of the great Rabon Gamaliel, a homiletic explanation from a rabbi next to a story of a mermaid by an old, experienced tar; a sketch of plant life by a simple farmer

EDUCATION AND THE TALMUD.

arrayed in line with an essay about medicinal anatomy by a famous medical sage. Not only Jews and early Jewish Christians are among its numberless contributors, but even pagans have acquired some place in its vast volumes. There are contributions from Sadducees, Epicureans, Romans, Persians, and Chaldeans, whose opinions are published even though they are not in harmony with the Talmudical faith or creed. The Talmud is a free trader in thought, its motto being "To know." It wants to know what the Almighty has done since he created the world, and is also eager to know what Rabbi Akiba did when he shut himself up privately with a noble Roman matron. It displays a fair method of criticism, free from any prejudice or favoritism, and there is not a saint on earth or an angel in heaven who is not made the target of the sharp arrows of true criticism. Even Moses is arraigned before the Talmudical bar, which criticises his conduct. Honor is given to whom honor is due, even though he be an opponent. Balaam, who was hired to curse the Jews, is, according to the Talmud, greater in prophecy than Moses.

The Rabbis, in dispute with Gentile sages, frankly admit the truth of the statements of the latter, if their arguments on the subject discussed were logical.

In poetry, the Talmud surpasses the Illiad of Homer, its vast volumes being one grand, long epic song, describing the heroic struggle of the giants of brain who fought the mighty gods of the mountains, as well as the gods of the valleys; the dreadful Druids, as well as the fearful demons. It is a tale of the struggle between light and darkness; between education and ignorance, with the final victory of the schoolmaster.

From an historical point of view, the Talmud may be taken as the record of historical deeds. We can get more information about the Hermit Kingdom of the Nile from it than from 10,000 mummified cats recently dug out from its shores at an enormous expense.

It is a pity that the Talmud has never been made accessible to the scientific world

I.—THE TWO TALMUDS.

Like the Hebrew religion, which is divided into two parts, the Elohistic and the Jehovistic cults, so the Talmud is divided into two parts, the Jerusalem Talmud and the Babylonian Talmud. In spite of the distinctive names there were many Babylonian contributors to the Jerusalem Talmud and many Jerusalem contributors to the Babylonian Talmud. From an educational standpoint, the Jerusalem Talmud is superior to that of Babylon, not only in age, but also in educational principles. The Jerusalem writers endeavored to train the tongue, while the Babylonians aimed to exercise the brain and mental faculties. Both Talmuds are prototypes of the two kinds of Jews, corresponding to the two kinds of religion. The Talmud of Jerusalem has a Jehovistic caste, with liberal toleration toward the Elohists, especially toward the early Jewish Christians, of whom many were in the ranks of its contributors. It is liberal, yet its liberality does not extend over the national border. It reminds one of Peterism of the early Christian period. The Babylonian Talmud has a broader view and has a cosmopolitan tendency, more like St. Paul. Like Paul, the Babylonian Talmud proclaims a heavenly Jerusalem, and, curiously enough, we there find the "missing link" between their views about non-Israelites. To the Babylonian Talmudist, as mentioned in former chapters, the pagan sage who studies the law is superior to the high priest who does not. Paul uttered the words: "If God wants children from Abraham, he can bring them forth from stones." Those who are acquainted with the methods of argument used in the Babylonian Talmud will find a striking resemblance between it and the arguments of Paul. Since Paul came from Tarshish, he must have had a Babylonian education; and also in the school of Gamaliel the Babylonian system was adopted, he (Gamaliel) having been one of the disciples of the great Babylonian, Hillel, whose deeds and teachings resemble those of Christ, who lived one hundred years later.

The Epistles of Peter are written in the style of the Jerusalem Talmud; he was probably trained after the Jerusalem method.

The Talmud of Jerusalem is like the Oriental Jew, while the Babylonian Talmud is the model of a Russian Jew in all his ways and manners.

The Jerusalem Talmud is written in a very plain style, leaving the impression that it was written by people of a high education, people who laid stress upon system and order—the indications of education. Its laws are paragraphed like a modern law book and its sentences are brief and to the point. More care is given to the rhetoric and drilling of the tongue than to the exercise of the brain. It lacks any speculation, and a dim gloom is cast upon it. The same can be said of the Oriental Jew, who is the outcome of his native Palestinian Talmud. To him, "words, words, and words" are more important than reason, and, like his Talmud, he moves in a narrow traditional circle of nationality. Like his Talmud, which condemns every speculation in physical research, he lacks that vigor of brain which has made the Occidental Hebrew, especially the Russian and Polish Jews, famous.

The Babylonian Talmud is the Eidolon of the Russian and the Polish Jew, with whom it grew near the Euphrates and the Tigris. The Russian and Polish Jews are descendants of the Babylonian Jews who entered Europe through Persia and the Caspian Sea. The Russian Jew is of an erratic nature, always of speculative turn, whether in matters of religion or matters of business. He is broad minded and sharp, yet his life is generally in a chaotic state, without order or system. If a Russian Jew is asked a question, instead of replying he will ask you another question, and in conversation he will take a long journey of talk until he at last wanders to the point. He will eat pork, yet, in spite of the fact that he is a lawbreaker, he will fast on the Atonement Day. He is a materialist in the full sense of the word, yet he possesses the mystic inclinations of a Mahatma. His Talmud (the Babylonian) is of the same character. In appearance, the Russian Jew is chaos itself. For him, every subject, no matter of how small importance, must be reasoned about, argued, and analyzed down to the last atomic substance until it is acknowledged as a law. In that respect he differs from Herbert Spencer, who says there is no chemistry for thought. When the Talmud begins to treat of a law—for instance, whether a ship is liable to house leprosy—it never comes to the point, but will wander through the Seven Heavens on high and the Seven Chambers of the Inferno until it comes back again to the starting point, and will then decide, after having employed all the resources of knowledge, that a ship is not a house.

The Babylonian Talmud might be likened to Faust, who wanted to be a saint in the heavenly Jerusalem and at the same time an Epicurean on the earth. It calls the Nazir, who vows to abstain from wine, a "sinner." Life, according to it, is a nuptial celebration, and is looked at from its brightest side. Even Satan appears therein as a gentleman. It approves of slang, which is expressive, though it often rises to the highest point in poetry. A sublime thought will be immediately followed by a vulgar expression, which fact once caused a refined millionaire, Ben Elasha, to leave the house of Jehuda at a nuptial feast. The Babylonian Talmud regards the exercise of the brain as superior to anything else, and he who can produce 150 reasons for purifying the rat, which Moses declared "unclean," is called a sage. He who would be a rabbi had to pass through such a brain examination before receiving his diploma. To speak in the words of the Talmud, they studied 300 kinds of laws upon the subject of "flying lower in the air" (could they have known of balloons?).

No matter how much the two Talmuds disagree, upon one point they agree—that education is the highest attainment of man; and both have mercilessly disfranchised the ignorant from many social rights to which any human being would naturally be entitled.

II.—DISFRANCHISEMENT OF THE IGNORANT.

The ignorant were, by the laws of the Talmud, expelled from the earthly social sphere, as well as from the heavenly, where a merciful God grants a shelter to any erring soul. Not only was he considered ignorant who could not himself read and

EDUCATION AND THE TALMUD. 1811

write, but he who had children and brought them up without education was also called ignorant. They were deprived of the following privileges:
1. No witness should be delivered to them, nor
2. Should they be accepted as such.
3. No secret should be told them.
4. They could not be appointed as apotropies (guardians) for orphans or managers of the charitable institutions.
5. They could not be taken as traveling companions.
6. What they lost could not be advertised (it was the custom to advertise "lost and found" articles through a herald).

A man, says the Talmud, who gives his daughter to an ignorant person does the same as though he bound her and gave her to a lion. Every calamity which comes upon a country is due only to the ignorant, according to Rabbinical ideas. A good illustration is found in the records of the Talmud, which shows to what a degree hatred against ignorance was carried: "Once," so says the Rabbinical history, "there was a famine in the land, and the benevolent, spiritual prince, Rabbi Jehuda, called the Saint, the editor of the Michna, opened his granaries with the notice that those who were versed either in the Scripture, or in the oral law, or in the folklore, or in any educational branch were invited to come and be fed. Rabbi Jonathan ben Amram forced his way in, and when he was asked by Rabbi Jehuda, 'Do you know the Scripture?' 'No,' was the reply. 'Do you know the oral law?' 'No,' he answered. He was given food, but when he went out the Rabbi groaned, saying, 'Woe to me, that I gave from my bread to one who was ignorant!'"

The ignorant person, says the Talmud, will not be resurrected. A man shall always sell all his belongings to marry the daughter of a sage. If not, let him marry the daughter of the president of a library or of a synagogue. If he can not find such, he shall try to marry the daughter of the president of the United Charity. If he can not find such, he shall marry the daughter of the schoolmaster, and not the daughter of an ignorant man. On the same page the Talmud declares that an ignorant person is not allowed by the law to eat any kind of meat. In another place it declares that the ignorant are out of place in society and unfit for witnesses. One rabbi went so far as to proclaim that if it were not for the sake of commerce the ignorant people ought to be killed. (This reminds one of Plato, who wanted in his Ideal State to have only able-bodied and able-minded citizens, while the rest were to be mercilessly shut out.)

In the same degree as the ignorant are despised, the wise are exalted. A sage who falls, says the oral law, should not have his shame made public. He who teaches the son of his friend knowledge, says the Talmud, will sometime be seated in the heavenly college of wisdom, and he who teaches the son of an ignorant person will have power to nullify even the decrees of the Almighty. A sage is, according to the Talmud, superior to the King of Israel, for if the sage dies we can hardly find one like him, but if the King dies every Israelite is fit for the position. The Talmud called the Persian Empire an "unworthy" one, because they had no national Alpha Beth and no grammar. (They adopted both of these from the cultured Medes.)

Everyone is requested by the oral law to salute a sage, even from the heathens, when passing by, by standing up. Rab. Diml, from Nahardai in Babylon, brought figs once in a boat to the market. The Exilearch (Reish Gola, the prince of the Exile) said to Raba, "Go and inquire if he is a learned man; then give the permit for the market." That illustrates what privileges the learned men enjoyed in the estimation of the editors of the Talmud. The Talmud even says that it would be better to neglect the service of the Lord than to give up the knowledge of the law.

RABBINICAL EDUCATIONAL LAWS.

In spite of the fact that the educational system of Palestine was different from that of Babylon, still, in the general outline of the laws concerning it, both had a uniform code, with slight alterations.

Every community was compelled by the law to maintain a kindergarten—"Makri Dardeki" (teacher of children). Besides these, the community was compelled by the law to maintain a penman, "Sofer" (scribe), whose duty it was to teach the children the art of writing.

A community was compelled to maintain:
1. A synagogue.
2. A beth hamidrash (a public library).
3. A bath house.
4. A kindergarten.
5. A public school.
6. A city penman.
7. A city physician.
8. A public toilet house.
9. A charitable institution.

In the community which had not the above institutions a learned man was not allowed to live.

The teachers of the kindergarten and of the public schools were paid by the city treasurer, who was under the control of the seven best men of the city (Shiwat Toboi Hair), corresponding to our modern city fathers. The colleges were maintained by donations from rich private professors and by college fees.

I.—The Teacher.

The teacher must be of good, moral reputation, and married. Bachelors and women were disqualified by the law from being teachers in public schools or in kindergartens. In regard to his pedagogic knowledge, the Palestinians laid more stress upon educational ability and in possessing a good method of pronunciation, while the Babylonians cared more for their learning. A Galilean was not qualified for the position of teacher in a public school, nor as a reader in the synagogue by the Palestinians, while in Babylon he could get such a position, provided he possessed the quality of learned speculation. Women were excluded from the pupil's bench as well as from the schoolmaster's chair. They could neither teach nor be taught, according to the Talmudical law.

II.—The Public Schools.

These were under the direct control of the city court in all matters pertaining to education, while the financial fairs were managed by the best seven elected men of the city. The schoolhouse, if it were not public property, was rented. The Rabbinical court never recognized the complaints of persons living near the school against the noise of the children which prevented them from sleeping. (It seems that they had night schools also.) The same complaint against the office of the city writer and the city physician was not recognized.

If a city was divided by a river or a stream, the parents were not compelled by the law to bring their children to the school "over the water," unless the bridge was broad and safe.

Makri Dardeki (The School of the Little Ones).—A general law of the Talmud says that when a child begins to talk its father is compelled to teach it. But there is a special Rabbinical educational standard which runs as follows: "At the age of 5, the child is to be taught reading; at the age of 10, Mishna (outlines of the oral law); at the age of 15, Talmud and universal knowledge. If the child was a healthy one, it was brought to the kindergarten at the age of 5. The class in that sort of school consisted of 25 pupils, and if there were 50 the city appointed another teacher, and if the class had only 40 pupils a helper was added. In that class the children were taught in a playing way to read the letters of the Alpha Beth in Babylonian on tablets of clay like those of the Chaldeans, and in Palestine even from rolls of parchment. The writing was required to be plain, simple, and readable, so that the

EDUCATION AND THE TALMUD.

child should know how to distinguish a dâleth (ד) from a résch (ר) which have a resemblance in the Hebrew letters.

At the age of 6 the child was brought into the public school under the care of the "Melamed Tinoketh" (teacher of children). In the Babylonian Talmud we have a record that Raw said to Rabbi Samuel bar Shiloth, who was a teacher in the public school, "At less than 6 years of age do not receive pupils; from 6 and upward feed him with reading matter like an ox." This is the most characteristic educational system of the Babylonians, who cared more for the accumulation of learning, regardless of a systematic order of education, than the Palestinians. The school children were allowed to read the weekly portions of the Bible by the light of the lamp on Sabbath night (which was prohibited to older people).

III.—PUNISHMENT.

Bodily punishment was prohibited in Palestine by an act of the fourth synod assembled on Awsha, and neither the parents nor the teachers were allowed to punish a child until the age of 12. The Babylonians had a light bodily punishment with shoestrings. It is mentioned in the Babylonian Talmud that Raw said to Rabbi Shiloth, who was a teacher in a public school, "When thou shalt punish a child, punish him with shoestrings."

IV.—VACATIONS.

A regular vacation for children was unknown to the Talmud rabbis. For them to learn to study was above all else. "Even for the sake of building the Temple, we do not allow the children to have a vacation," says the Talmud; "and Jerusalem," claims the same book, "was destroyed because they often permitted the schoolmasters to be idle." "The world only exists for the sake of the little ones," says the Talmud. With the exception of the hours for prayer and the festivals, which required the presence of the children, their study went on without pause or rest. Often in times of calamity, as in times of pestilence and cholera, the schools were closed. It was a custom, when the country suffered from drought, to order a fast day, when the children were brought to the market place, where open prayer meetings were held, and the people implored the Most High in sackcloth and ashes, pointing to the little ones, praying, "O Lord, hear us and give us grace for the sake of these school children, who are pure from sin."

On Sabbaths and other feast days the subjects of study were of light matters—for little children, reading exercises; for college boys, homiletics.

EDUCATIONAL DUTIES OF PARENTS.

The educational duties of the parents were four in number:

(a) The father's duty is, by the law, to bring up and rear his children (the male ones) on all the branches of knowledge, even in national folklore.

(b) The father's duty is to teach his son a trade.

(c) The father is even compelled to teach his son how to swim.

(d) The father is to care for his son's religious training and education.

These are the duties of a grandfather to be fulfilled to his grandchild.

The mother's duty was only one, namely, to bring her children into the school-house and to the prayer meeting.

RELIGIOUS EDUCATION.

"Religious training" is not to be found on the calendar of education, yet it is the most important item in it, and the Talmud has separated that part, placing it in the hands of the parents that they may educate that part of the child which is out of the reach of the schoolmaster, ennobling the inner feelings and the emotions of the soul. That portion of the education was in the hands of the parents, principally the father. The Talmud says that we shall accustom the child to the duties of the laws, even to accustom it to fast. The religious training was conducted at home, not in the school. The child, by virtue of his childish notions, like all children, was eager to know about any strange ceremony which took place in the religious domestic life. For instance, the child asked the meaning of the "Mezuza" (a sort of talisman which Moses requested them to put on the doorposts). The father then explained to the child its meaning as well as its historical advent. Every feast day was an opportunity for the father to give a religious instruction to his son on that subject. For instance, at the Feast of the Tabernacles, when the family removed from the house to live for a week in a tent, the child, of course, was eager to know why, and so the father explained the reason from a religious point of view. On the night of the Passover, before the proceedings of the feast, the child asked four questions of his father in regard to the curious customs in that peculiar feast. That custom still prevails among the Polish and Orthodox Jews. The Talmud says that on the night of the Passover nuts and fruits were given to the children in order that they should be awake and listening to the history of the exodus from Egypt.

The child, according to the Jewish view, is not responsible for the religious law until the age of 13, when he is no longer a minor in religious matters. But there is one duty resting upon the shoulders of the child regardless of his age, to which he is subjected, and that is the kadish (sanctification). The kadish is a short prayer, like the Lord's Prayer, and is distinguished from other prayers, as it is said in the very ancient Aramaic language. Its antiquity is beyond any doubt. The kadish is to the Jews what the mass is to the Catholics. If one of the parents dies the child is brought morning and evening into the synagogue to recite the kadish during the first twelve months, in loving remembrance of his departed father or mother. After the elapse of the first year, the kadish is recited by the child or by the grown son each year on the day of the death of the father or the mother. The kadish can only be recited in the presence of 10 male worshipers. Even a female child is subjected to the duty of the kadish. The kadish is calculated to implant into the heart of the child the noblest seeds of gratitude, and it is a very old custom, a transfiguration of the primitive "ancestor worship." What an impression must the Rabbinical lore make upon the sensitive heart of the child, by declaring that when the child recites the kadish, and the worshipers say "Amen," the soul of the departed father or mother, to whose memory the kadish was said, is released from purgatory. The kadish is the only custom still common among all the Jews, no matter whether Reform or Orthodox. You can even find Jews who have thrown overboard the whole Mosaic religion, yet, on the day of death of their parents they will search for 10 male worshipers, and pay them for their time, in order to be able to recite in their presence the kadish. Here we see the powerful effect of that religious training. Why? Because the kadish touches the most delicate threads of the human heart, and it is not merely a religious, but a humane instinct of mankind.

On the same principle of gratitude, the child was compelled by the law, to be enforced by the father, to say the benediction after each meal and to invoke a blessing before tasting any kind of fruit.

BABYLONIAN EDUCATION.

The Babylonians, although in many respects superior to the Palestinians, as they lived in a country which had been a seat of culture from immemorial times, were inferior in regard to education in its full sense and meaning.

The Babylonians were great thinkers, but very poor philosophers. They had an education, but not a pedagogic one. They had a system, but no order. They know all the languages spoken in the celestial realm, but were very poor linguists in the tongues spoken on the terrestrial sphere. They had school laws, but no regulations, and those which they had were methods and systems adopted from the Palestinians. The Babylonians adopted the kindergarten after the Palestinian model many centuries later than its use began in Palestine. Nevertheless, we will sketch their method,

EDUCATION AND THE TALMUD.

although the execution of the regulations were different from those of Palestine. In Palestine, for instance, corporal punishment was prohibited, and even a parent could not make use of the strap until after the age of 12. Now, there is a peculiar case recorded in the Babylonian Talmud where a teacher violated that regulation and was left unpunished, as it seems that in Babylon the shoestring was the regulator. The case in question is as follows: The father of the later famous Samuel found him weeping. He asked him, "My child, why do you cry?" He replied, "My schoolmaster kicked me." "For what?" asked his father. "Because I did not wash the hands of his son when I gave him something to eat." "Why did you not?" The child answered, "He eats and I shall wash my hands?" The father simply remarked that it was not enough that the teacher was ignorant of the law (which requires hand washing only if he eats), and he also slapped him. From that case it seems that the Babylonians tolerated the injustice of the teachers. In regard to the methods and application of teaching it was in the "Makri Dardeky" (the reading of the little ones) of the simplest manner.

ILLUSTRATION OF METHODS EMPLOYED.

The child at the age of 5 went to the "Makri Dardeky," which corresponds to our modern kindergarten. The term was one year and the class only 25 children. If more came, helpers were appointed. As in our modern kindergartens, where the children acquire the quantities of words in a playing manner without any mental strain, so in the Hebrew "Makri Dardeki" the child accumulated many words and ideas of domestic use in a pleasant way, without any mental effort. The character of the letters of the Hebrew Alpha Beth is that of an unpainted picture book, and the Alpha Beth was used for that purpose. The child was shown the two-horned letter Aleph א, which means "the Bull," the leader, the teacher. The next letter, Beth ב, means a house, as its figure resembles the primitive houses. The third letter, Gimel ג, means a camel, while the letter D or Dalit ד, means a door, because its shape resembles a door; and the letter S or Sain ץ resembles a sword, with the collective meaning of "weapons," "arms," etc.

Besides words and their various meanings and applications acquired by the letters of the whole Alpha Beth during the period of one year, the child also learned to number, as the letters of the Alpha Beth, like those of the Latin, are also signs for numerals.

METHODS EMPLOYED BY THE MELAMED TINOKETH, OR IN THE PUBLIC SCHOOLS.

In the public school, under the direction of the "Melamed Tinoketh" (children's teacher), the Alpha Beth was also used in the first standard, its letters serving as poetical reading matter, the purpose being to awaken the desire of knowledge in the child, and to rouse his feelings for all that is good and noble.

The methods employed bear the stamp of simplicity, yet had great effective force. The child was taught that Aleph Beth means "Learn wisdom" (Aleph means learn; Beth is the first initial of Bina, wisdom). Gimel (g), Dalit (d), it was explained, as to help the poor. (Gimel means to reward, to extend grace and mercy; Dalit means those in poverty.) The teacher would explain that the reason the face of the Gimel was toward the back of the Dalith (in the Alpha Beth, reading from right to left, as ד (d) ג (g), was that the good man must always hunt up the poor in order to help them. Why is the face of the Dalith turned away from the Gimel? In order to receive the alms secretly, so as not to be ashamed. The next letters were explained as how God would reward the good, and is always willing to receive the wicked if he repents. The R (ר) is the initial of Racha (meaning the wicked). The K (כ) is the initial of Kadosh, the Holy One. Why is the face of the K toward the R? Because the Holy One looks after the wicked that he may repent. The Alpha Beth in the rank and file of its letters was explained to the child in its esoteric meaning.

The teacher also often combined them. For instance, the first letter, Aleph, with the last letter, Taw, and explained the combination.

The Alpha Beth served as a first reader, and the explanations were calculated to educate first the man in the child, and then the Jewish religious spirit. The Shin (ש) and the Taw (ח), for instance, were explained to the child thus: Why is the Shin, the initial of Sheka (falsehood), resting only on one stem, while the Taw rests on two? Because falsehood can not stand long, while truth stands forever.

Foreseeing the difficulties which grown students would have to encounter in later years, in facing the various contradictions, controversies, and explanations which are always the source of doubt, leading the student astray, the education was arranged to make such impressions upon the child as to form a guide in the religious labyrinth, by the aid of the Alpha Beth, which served as the first reader. The M, for instance, has a double letter, one called the "open" M ('ס), and it is written at the beginning and in the middle of words. The other is termed the "closed" M ([ ]), and is written only at the end of words. Now, the teacher explained that the M which is the initial for Mamar (word, logos) that there is an open word and a hidden word, meaning that each sentence has an open meaning according to the plain words, and another hidden meaning, requiring a deeper study and understanding independent of the language and grammar. By such an educational method the child grew up with that impression, and, as a grown man was prevented from stumbling over the contradictions and unexplainable sentences.

In the public school the child spent from the age of 5 to the age of 10, during which time he acquired the perfect reading with the vowels and punctuations, composition, the art of writing (which was taught by the Lawler, or city penman), grammar, and homiletic explanations of the Scripture.

At the age of 10 the boy was well versed in the Bible from the first chapter of Genesis to the last of Malachi, until he knew the whole by heart and was able to construct sensible compositions without faults, when he was ripe to enter the first standard of the college where the Mishna, a brief outline of the oral law, was taught.

It was not customary to have a vacation in the public school, and the Talmud tells us that Rab Samuel bar Shiloth, who was a public school teacher, had not seen his own orchard for thirteen years, as he could not get leave of absence.

TITLES AND TERMS.

The word "teacher" has three terms in the Hebrew language, corresponding to the three different positions they occupied in the Hebrew world.

The first is Melamed, a term which means a goad, and is translated as the oxgoad. This was applied to the teacher of the public schools, Melamed Tinoketh, teacher of children, as they were goaded by the rigid will of discipline of the teacher.

The second term is Moro, which denotes the guide, the pointer, and the word often comes in connection with road, path. The same term was applied to the college professor and to the judge, who had only to point out the way or road which should be trod.

The third term was Aluf, a word meaning a bull, or steer, who goes before the flock. It means the leader, the prince, the king (in Arabic, the Chaliph). It means also the unit of thousand (elef), and in the Chaldean jargon, to learn. This term was applied to the director of a college or to a distinguished public man who led the people in any way. The penman who taught the art of writing, from the point of the pen, was called in the Talmudic, Chaldaic jargon, Lawler, meaning plain, penman, while the poet, or teacher of writing of a higher degree, was called Sofer, a term which means the teller, the counter, the scribe. Ezra had the title of Sofer.

Books were called the Megiloth, rolls, and Sefarim, the singular number being Sofer. It is curious that the term of Sofer, book, is mentioned in the five books of Moses, while in the prophets the term Megiloth, rolls, is to be found.

EDUCATION AND THE TALMUD.

The pen was called "et," a term which means hidden, veiled. It has the same meaning as cheret (the instrument used by the hieroglyphists in Egypt for engraving their mysterious writings).

My friend, Judge Sulzberger, called my attention to the similarity in sound between the familiar English word, "etching," and "et," in Hebrew, and chrat, engraving, and the English "cut." The term "et" (pen) was used in the primitive times, when writing was not common, and the Levite poet who dedicated a psalm (Ps. 45) to King Solomon on his nuptial day prefaces his poem with the explanation that his tongue is of the et, or pen, is that of a diligent Sofer, writer-poet.

Later, about the time of the prophets, when the art of writing was more common and had spread among the people, they called the pen, in a poetical way, koseth, which means bow, like kesheth. They then began to understand the power of the pen, which was compared to the bow, and its letters to shooting arrows. The prophet Ezekiel describes the angel who was sent to mark the foreheads of the wicked dedicated to destruction as being armed with the bow of the writer on his loin (Ezekiel, ix, 4).

It was, and is still among the Orientals, the custom to wear the pen girdled on the loins like a weapon.

The pupil was called Talmid, or the disciplined one. The wandering scholars, who, according to the statements of the Talmud, wandered from place to place to teach, were called Talmide chachamin (disciples of sages). It reminds one of the wandering scalds and minnesingers of the Odin school, whom the poet Von Schöffel has immortalized as the "fahrende Schüler," wandering scholars.

A learned man who was not connected with any college had the title of Chaber, which means fellow, and the relation of fellowship to the college was of the same character as the English fellowship to Oxford and Cambridge.

The title of Chaber was also applied to the magician of the Persian type, or a snake tamer.

The graduate of a college received the title of Rabbi, a title which was applied to any leader of any union of workmen; even to the leader of the hangmen, who had a union among themselves. The title of Rabbi did not entitle its possessor to preach or teach.

The judge or the student who devoted his time to the study of law, civil or religious, was given the title of Dajon, judge.

An astronomer, or any learned man in a special branch of knowledge, was called a Chaldean sage, while the special medical man had the title of Chakim (the same as in Arabic to-day). The Talmud often calls him "Asje" (healer), probably after the name of the Essicians, that famous sect whose main object was to heal, and of whom Christ was a member (Essenes).

The title of Rabon (our master) was applied to the hereditary spiritual prince, who was elective also, and often the power was taken from him and placed in the hands of another.

The title of Rabon was also applied to various others beside the hereditary princes. Gamaliel, the teacher of St. Paul, had the title of Rabon Gamliel. The higher grade of Rabon was the mention of the simple name, as Hillel, who was the spiritual prince Nasi is always mentioned by his simple name, Hillel, as the highest title; hence, Moses and the prophets are mentioned only by their proper simple names. The ranks of the doubles or pairs who succeeded the Great Synod are mentioned by their names as well as the names of their fathers, as Simon ben Sotath (the son of Sotath). The name of the father was added to that of any distinguished person who merited his fame by any great public reform, such as the great educator and high priest Jehoshua ben Gamla. If a sage was unmarried (which was an obstacle in the way of holding office) or some faults were found in him, he was mentioned simply as the son of this or that, as ben Asi, ben Soma—i. e., the son of Asi, the son of Soma. Both their names were Simon, but were omitted on account of their being bachelors and philosophers.

Synonyms are often used in the Talmud, as well as nicknames. The titles were bestowed by the professors of the colleges, and the document was written and testified to by the college seal.

The early authors of the Talmud are called Tanaim (legislators), the later contributors Amoraim (a term which means sea captains, who knew how to swim in the vast ocean of the Talmud). The term also means explainer, as they explained the laws of the Tanaim, or legislators. Those contributors who lived before the final close of the Talmud had the titles of Rabanou Saburai (rabbis of explanations). In Babylon the title of the spiritual prince was Reish Gola, the head of the exile, who got his title through hereditary election and indorsement by the Persian King. The Reish Golas, or the Exilearchs, were far inferior to the spiritual princes of Palestine, although the former executed a more forcible power. The professor of the college in Babylon had the title of Rosh Jeshiba, head of the sitting, as in previous times the students had listened standing to the lectures, and when this custom was abolished they called the college the "sitting."

When the Exilarchy was abolished, a new title was instituted, Gaon, or exalted, a title which was not appended to any office, except as the mark of great learning. One of the most noted of the exalted ones was Rabbi Saadjo Gaon, the thousandth anniversary of whose death was celebrated recently in the Jewish world.

The title of Gaon was conferred upon every Jew on the Asiatic and African continents, and on a few of the Spanish Jews who were rabbis during the Moorish reign. Among the European rabbis, only one, Rabbi Elijah Gaon, from Vilna, in Russia, who lived in the eighteenth century, enjoyed the title, and is still mentioned as "the Gaon."

FROM THE GREAT SYNOD UP TO THE TIME OF JEHOSHUA BEN GAMLA, THE HIGH PRIEST, OR EDUCATIONAL HISTORY OF PALESTINE.

When the Great Synod assembled at the call of Ezra the Scribe, the session lasted nearly a century, one of its members being the high priest, Simon the Righteous, who lived at the time when Alexander the Great invaded Palestine.

The work of reorganization was a tremendous one, and the synod had to battle with difficulties of numberless obstacles. The condition of Palestine after the return was not very favorable. Most of the villages were mere piles of ruins; the husbandry was in a state of perfect neglect; the country was overrun with tramps and robbers and other kindred vagabonds; the bulk of the 50,000 who returned from the exile were very poor and ignorant. But the most dangerous foe they had to battle with was the Samaritans, who showed an ugly attitude of hostility toward the Great Synod, and the delay of the building of the Temple was due only to the Samaritans who wrote slanderous letters to the kings of Persia, who had a protectorate over Palestine. In spite of all these difficulties the synod proceeded from the beginning to enact educational laws, as only through them did they hope to revive the ancient national spirit, and improve the material condition of the country. The first law on the educational code was to make the father responsible for the education of his male children; the second law was to establish schools in Jerusalem, maintained by the public treasury of the Temple. As the people for safety flocked to Jerusalem, and the building of the Temple drew a multitude of laborers, the city soon became very populous and strengthened. As soon as the building of the Temple was finished, people flocked to Palestine from the neighboring States and countries, from Egypt, Arabia, and Asia Minor. These people brought with them not only material wealth, but also the culture and civilization of the countries from which they came. Jerusalem was restored and made a national center, from which as a basis operations were extended throughout Palestine to root out those tramps and highwaymen. Order began to prevail, villages sprang up, and husbandry flourished again around the beautiful plains of En Gedi. Hand in hand with the national material progress went marching onward the educational spirit, and the educator

EDUCATION AND THE TALMUD.

did the same pioneer work as the soldier. By breaking up the priestly hierarchy and by creating new offices, as the supreme court, the sanhedrim, consisting of 71 members, and the creation of the little sanhedrim for the provinces, consisting of 23 members, and the justice of the peace (beth din), of 3 members for every town, the Synod opened new avenues for the laity, spurred on by the educational spirit. (The Sanhedrim sat in the marble chamber in the Temple, having the jurisdiction over the whole nation and controlling all the educational departments and the public treasury of the Temple. No war could be declared without the sanction of that body. Trials of national importance, as that of a king or of the priest or the trial of an individual, which was of national importance, were held before the sanhedrim. The famous trial of Christ was before that body).

Outside of the Temple gate was the seat of the little sanhedrim, as in the capitals of each respective province that body was empowered to pass the death sentence in murder cases. The beth din, or the court of justice, in each town tried only civil cases.

The great knowledge, sacred as well as profane, required by the law of every office seeker, indirectly compelled them to visit schools and obtain the diploma of professor of well-reputed colleges. After the dissolution of the Great Synod, its legislative power was invested in the Sanhedrim, and from time to time synods were called to assemble when some great reform was in view.

At the time of Simon ben Sotach, who lived in the year 105 B. C., and was the president of the Great Sanhedrim and the brother-in-law of King Janai, was made the rigid law that every child must attend the school. The Babylonian Talmud gives the credit of that law to the high priest Jehoshua ben Gamla, who lived in the year 65 B. C., and was executed later by the Zealots. In history the Babylonian Talmud is unreliable, as the Babylonians had a prejudice against the Palestinians and the Alexandrians, so the attitude of the Bablyonian Talmud toward Christ is different from that of the Jerusalem Talmud. No wonder that the name of Simon ben Sotach is not mentioned in the Babylonian Talmud, which has a great prejudice against his brother-in-law, the king, who, according to its narrative, was killing the sages, facts not mentioned in the Talmud of Jerusalem. The Babylonian Text concerning education runs as follows:

"For good shall be remembered the name of that man Jehoshua ben Gamla, for only for his sake the law has been preserved thus far; he who was able brought his child to Jerusalem to attend school, or he whose father was a learned man was taught the law too. So they legislated to establish schools in every capital of the respective provinces. But as this was still insufficient Jehoshua ben Gamla legislated that the children from 6 years of age must attend school in each city, town, or village."

The fact that Simon ben Sotach is not mentioned is rather surprising, and many have tried to make it appear that Simon ben Sotach legislated only for the provincial capitals while Jehoshua ben Gamla extended the law to all communities. From both Talmuds it would seem that they were not the lawmakers, but only enforced the laws already existing in regard to education in a rigid manner—as is often the case with many laws at various times in different ages and in almost every country. Why the Babylonian Talmud does not mention Simon ben Sotach and the Talmud of Jerusalem does not mention the martyr Jehoshua ben Gamla have both an inner historical reason.

At the near approach of the close of the Great Synod, Jerusalem was peopled by nearly a million inhabitants, more than the whole population of the rest of the country at that time, hence the first educational laws legislated by the synod were those relating to suffrage for the whole country, for at that time it could be said that all Palestine was in Jerusalem, as in the seventeenth and eighteenth centuries it was said that all France was in Paris.

The historical evidences of the great educational power are: The six divisions of the Mishna, the two great encyclopedias of the two Talmuds, with the numberless tractats of the Medrashim (college periodicals). Besides that vast literature, which deals with every imaginable branch of science, there were books and booklets, written at the time of the second Temple, of which all have been lost and only their authors are mentioned in the Talmuds, as "Megilath Chasidim" (book of the pious), probably the Talmud of the Essenes.

The book of Tiglath ben Lana, which the Talmud places among the Apocrypha (I believe the name of the author was only a pseudonym for one of the Apostles), "Megilath Setarim" (the Roll of the Mysteries), probably a cabalistic code, "Megiloth Jachsin" (the Roll of Genealogy), a book which was written in the style of the Biblical Chronicle, and from which the Palestinians refused to teach the Babylonians. The Apocrypha is another classical work of the time of the second Temple, whose authors tried to imitate the style and method of writing of the primitive authors of the Bible.

CHAPTER XLVII.
PUBLICATIONS OF THE UNITED STATES BUREAU OF EDUCATION.

[From 1867 to 1895.]

1. Annual Report of the Commissioner of Education, 1867–68. Barnard. 8°. pp. xl+856.
2. Special Report of the Commissioner of Education on the condition and improvement of public schools in the District of Columbia. Barnard. 8°. pp. 912. Washington, 1871. (Reprinted as Barnard's Am. Jour. of Education, vol. 19.)
3. Annual Report of the Commissioner of Education for the year 1870. Eaton. 8°. pp. 579. Washington, 1870.
4. ——— 1871. Eaton. 8°. pp. 715. Washington, 1872.
5. ——— 1872. Eaton. 8°. pp. lxxxviii+1018. Washington, 1873.
6. ——— 1873. Eaton. 8°. pp. clxxviii+870. Washington, 1874.
7. ——— 1874. Eaton. 8°. pp. clii+935. Washington, 1875.
8. ——— 1875. Eaton. 8°. pp. clxxiii+1016. Washington, 1876.
9. ——— 1876. Eaton. 8°. pp. ccxiii+942. Washington, 1878.
10. ——— 1877. Eaton. 8°. pp. ccvi+641. Washington, 1879.
11. ——— 1878. Eaton. 8°. pp. ccl+730. Washington, 1880.
12. ——— 1879. Eaton. 8°. pp. ccxxx+757. Washington, 1881.
13. ——— 1880. Eaton. 8°. pp. cclxii+914. Washington, 1882.
14. ——— 1881. Eaton. 8°. pp. cclxxvii+840. Washington, 1883.
15. ——— 1882–83. Eaton. 8°. pp. ccxciii+872. Washington, 1884.
16. ——— 1883–84. Eaton. 8°. pp. cclxxi+943. Washington, 1885.
17. ——— 1884–85. Eaton-Dawson. 8°. pp. cccxvii+848. Washington, 1886.
18. ——— 1885–86. Dawson. 8°. pp. xxi+792. Washington, 1887.
19. ——— 1886–87. Dawson. 8°. pp. 1170. Washington, 1888.
20. ——— 1887–88. Dawson. 8°. pp. 1209. Washington, 1888.
21. Illiteracy, derived from census tables of 1860; Educational statistics, translation of article by Dr. A. Ficker; Virchow on schoolroom diseases; Education of French and Prussian conscripts; School organization, etc. pp. 70. (Circ. inf. August, 1870.)
22. Public instruction in Sweden and Norway; The "folkehoiskoler" of Denmark. By C. C. Andrews. pp. 48. (Circ. inf. July, 1871.)
23. Methods of school discipline. By Hiram Orcutt. pp. 14. (Circ. inf. November, 1871.)
24. Compulsory education. By L. Van Bokkelen. pp. 17. (Circ. inf. December, 1871.)
25. German and other foreign universities. By Herman Jacobson. pp. 43. (Circ. inf. January, 1872.)
26. Public instruction in Greece, the Argentine Republic, Chile, and Ecuador; Statistics respecting Portugal and Japan; Technical education in Italy. By John M. Francis, George John Ryan, F. M. Tanaka. pp. 77. (Circ. inf. February, 1882.)
27. Vital statistics of college graduates; Distribution of college students in 1870–71; Vital statistics in the United States, with diagrams. By Charles Warren. pp. 93. (Circ. inf. March, 1872.)
28. Relation of education to labor. By Richard J. Hinton. pp. 125. (Circ. inf. April, 1872.)
29. Education in the British West Indies. By Thomas H. Pearne. pp. 22. (Circ. inf. June, 1872.)
30. The Kindergarten. By Baroness Marenholtz-Bülow, tr. by Elizabeth P. Peabody. pp. 62. (Circ. inf. July, 1872.)
31. American education at the Vienna Exposition of 1873. pp. 79. (Circ. inf. November, 1872.)
32. Historical summary and reports on the systems of public instruction in Spain, Bolivia, Uruguay, and Portugal. pp. 66. (Circ. inf. 1, 1873.)
33. Schools in British India. By Joseph Warren. pp. 30. (Circ. inf. 2, 1873.)
34. College commencements for the summer of 1873, in Maine, New Hampshire, Vermont, Massachusetts, Rhode Island, Connecticut, New York, New Jersey, and Pennsylvania. pp. 118. (Circ. inf. 3, 1873.)

1821

35. List of publications by members of certain college faculties and learned societies in the United States, 1867-1872. pp. 72. (Circ. inf. 4, 1873.)
36. College commencements during 1873 in the Western and Southern States. pp. 155. (Circ. inf. 5, 1873.)
37. Proceedings of the Department of Superintendence of the National Educational Association, Washington, D. C. (1874). pp. 77. (Circ. inf. 1, 1874.)
   Partial contents: Uniform plan and form for publishing the principal statistical tables on education, by George J. Lucky; Scientific and industrial education and the true policy of the National and State Government in regard to it, by Hon. A. D. White; The International Centennial Exposition as a world-wide educator, by W. D. Kelley; Report by the committee on the relations of the General Government to education in the District of Columbia.
38. Drawing in public schools; present relation of art to education in the United States. By Isaac Edwards Clarke. pp. 56. (Circ. inf. 2, 1874.)
39. History of secondary instruction in Germany. By Herman Jacobson. pp. 87. (Circ. inf. 3, 1874.)
40. Proceedings of the Department of Superintendence of the National Educational Association, Washington, D. C. (1875). pp. 114. (Circ. inf. 1, 1875.)
   Partial contents: The legal prevention of illiteracy, by B. G. Northrop; Brain culture in relation to the schoolroom, by A. N. Bell; The origin of the alphabet, by Prof. J. Enthoffer; American education at the Centennial Exposition, by J. P. Wickersham; Can the elements of industrial education be introduced into our common schools? by John D. Philbrick; Industrial drawing in public schools, by Prof. Walter Smith.
41. Education in Japan. By William E. Griffis. pp. 64. (Circ. inf. 2, 1875.)
42. Public Instruction in Belgium, Russia, Turkey, Servia, and Egypt. By Emile de Laveleye, M. de Salve, V. E. Dor. pp. 103. (Circ. inf. 3, 1875.)
43. Waste of labor in the work of education. By Paul A. Chadburne. pp. 10. (Circ. inf. 4, 1875
44. Educational exhibit at the International Centennial Exhibition, 1876. pp. 26. (Circ. inf. 5, 1875.)
45. Reformatory, charitable, and industrial schools for the young. By Julia A. Holmes and S. A. Martha Canfield. pp. 208. (Circ. inf. 6, 1875.)
46. Constitutional provisions in regard to education in the several States. By Franklin Hough. pp. 130. (Circ. inf. 7, 1875.)
47. Schedule for the preparation of students' work for the Centennial Exhibition. By A. J. Rickoff, J. L. Pickard, James H. Smart (committee). pp. 15. (Circ. inf. 8, 1875.)
48. Education in China. By William A. P. Martin. pp. 28. (Circ. inf. 1, 1877.)
49. Public Instruction in Finland, the Netherlands, Denmark, Würtemberg, and Portugal; the University of Leipzig. By Felix Heikel, C. H. Pinggé, and J. L. Corning. pp. 77. (Circ. inf. 2, 1877.)
50. Training of teachers in Germany. pp. 36. (Circ. inf. 1, 1878.)
51. Elementary education in London, with address of Sir Charles Reed. pp. 24. (Circ. inf. 2, 1878.)
52. Training schools for nurses. By S. A. Martha Canfield. pp. 21. (Circ. inf. 1, 1879.)
53. Proceedings of the Department of Superintendence of the National Educational Association, 1877 and 1879, Washington, D. C.; Proceedings of the conference of college presidents and delegates, Columbus, Ohio, December, 1877. pp. 102. (Cir. inf. 2, 1879.)
   Partial contents: Proceedings of 1877: The school organization of a State; National aid to education. What has been done by the General Government in aid of education, by John Eaton; General appropriation of public lands; Proceeds of sales of public lands; Disposition of surplus revenue by States; American education, by George B. Loving; The high school question, by James H. Smart.
   Partial contents: Proceedings of 1879: Popular education in Switzerland, by John Hitz; Popular education in France, by E. C. Wines; Technical education, by E. A. Apgar; Kindergarten training, by Louise Pollock; Education in the South, by G. J. Orr; The needs of the United States Bureau of Education; Instruction in governmental ideas, by Wm. Strong; Technical education and industrial drawing, by Walter Smith; Education at the Paris Exposition, by John D. Philbrick; What has been done by the National Government in aid of education, by John Eaton; American education, by George B. Loving; The high school question, by James H. Smart; Collegiate degrees, by John M. Gregory.
   Partial contents: Proceedings of the conference of the presidents and other delegates of the State universities and State colleges of Ohio for 1877: Collegiate degrees, by J. M. Gregory; Scientific studies and courses of study; Report on the military system in State colleges, by Edward Orton.
54. Value of common school education to common labor. (Reprinted from Annual Report, 1872.) pp. 37. (Circ. inf. 3, 1879.)
55. Training schools for cookery. By S. A. Martha Canfield. pp. 49. (Circ. inf. 4, 1879.)
56. American education as described by the French commission to the International Exhibition of 1876. By Ferdinand Buisson and others. pp. 37. (Circ. inf. 5, 1879.)

PUBLICATIONS OF THE BUREAU OF EDUCATION. 1823

57. College libraries as aids to instruction. By Justin Winsor and Otis H. Robinson. pp. 27. (Circ. inf. 1, 1880.)
58. Proceedings of the Department of Superintendence of the National Educational Association, Washington, D. C., 1880. pp. 112. (Circ. inf. 2, 1880.)
    Partial contents: Bell's system of visible speech, by L. A. Butterfield; Education of dependent children, by C. D. Randall; Best system of schools for a State, by J. H. Smart; University education, by David C. Gilman; Technical education in its relations to elementary schools, by J. D. Philbrick; Technological museums, by J. D. Philbrick; The Tenth Census from an educational point of view, by W. T. Harris; Discussion of the high school question, by J. W. Dickinson, W. T. Harris, J. P. Wickersham; Congress and the education of the people, by W. H. Ruffner; Laws relating to the State public school for dependent children at Coldwater, Michigan. Outline of the school systems of the various States.
59. Legal rights of children. By S. M. Wilcox. pp. 96. (Circ. inf. 3, 1880.)
60. Rural school architecture. By T. M. Clark. pp. 106. (Circ. inf. 4, 1880.)
61. English rural schools. By Henry W. Hulbert. pp. 26. (Circ. inf. 5, 1880.)
62. Instruction in chemistry and physics in the United States. By F. W. Clarke. pp. 219. (Circ. inf. 6, 1880.)
63. The spelling reform. By Francis A. March. pp. 36. (Circ. inf. 7, 1880.)
64. Construction of library buildings. By William F. Poole. pp. 26. (Circ. inf. 1, 1881.)
65. Relation of education to industry and technical training in American schools. By E. E. White. pp. 22. (Circ. inf. 2, 1881.)
66. Proceedings of the Department of Superintendence of the National Educational Association, New York, 1881, pp. 79. (Circ. inf. 3, 1881.)
    Partial contents: Uniformity of school statistics, by Andrew McMillan; The conservation of pedagogic energy, by C. O. Thompson; Our schools and our forests, by Franklin B. Hough; Museums illustrative of education, by John Eaton; Education and the State, by J. W. Patterson.
67. Education in France. pp. 144. (Circ. inf. 4, 1881.)
68. Causes of deafness among school children, and the instruction of children with impaired hearing. By Samuel Sexton. pp. 47. (Circ. inf. 5, 1881.)
69. Effects of student life on the eyesight. By A. W. Calhoun. pp. 29. (Circ. inf. 6, 1881.)
70. Inception, organization, and management of training schools for nurses. By S. A. Martha Canfield. pp. 28. (Circ. inf. 1, 1882.)
71. Proceedings of the Department of Superintendence of the National Educational Association, Washington, 1882. pp. 112. (Circ. inf. 2, 1882.)
    Partial contents: Information necessary to determine the merits of the heating and ventilation of a school building, by John S. Billings, U. S. A.; The chemical examination of air as applied to questions of ventilation, by Dr. Charles Smart, U. S. A.; Obstacles in the way of better primary education, by H. Jones; Chairs of pedagogy in our higher institutions of learning, by G. Stanley Hall; National aid to education, from a Northern standpoint, by Dexter H. Hawkins; Education in Alaska, by Sheldon Jackson; Resolution respecting a national appropriation for education in Alaska; Some fundamental inquiries concerning the common-school studies, by John M. Gregory; How to improve the qualifications of teachers, by W. T. Harris.
72. University of Bonn. By Edmond Dreyfus-Brisac. pp. 67. (Circ. inf. 3, 1882.)
73. Industrial art in schools. By Charles G. Leland. pp. 37. (Circ. inf. 4, 1882.)
74. Maternal schools in France. pp. 14. (Circ. inf. 5, 1882.)
75. Technical instruction in France. pp. 63. (Circ. inf. 6, 1882.)
76. Legal provisions respecting the examination and licensing of teachers. pp. 46. (Circ. inf. 1, 1883.)
77. Coeducation of the sexes in the public schools of the United States. pp. 30. (Circ. inf. 2, 1883.)
78. Proceedings of the Department of Superintendence of the National Educational Association, Washington, D. C., 1883. pp. 81. (Circ. inf. 3, 1883.)
    Partial contents: Natural history in public schools, its utility and practicability as illustrated by the methods adopted in New York City, by Albert S. Bickmore; Communication respecting industrial education, by Chas. G. Leland; The educational lessons of the census, by Wm. T. Harris; If universal suffrage, then universal education, by Atticus G. Haygood; Constitutionality of national aid to education, by Wm. Lawrence; Indian education, by B. G. Northrop, S. C. Armstrong, Alice C. Fletcher; School supervision: How and by whom the fitness of pupils for promotion is determined, by C. G. Edwards and others.
79. Recent school-law decisions. By Lyndon A. Smith. pp. 82. (Circ. inf. 4, 1883.)
80. Meeting of the International Prison Congress at Rome. pp. 11. (Circ. inf. 1, 1884.)
81. The teaching, practice, and literature of shorthand. (Second and enlarged edition.) By Julius E. Rockwell. pp. 184. (Circ. inf. 2, 1884.)
82. Illiteracy in the United States. With appendix on national aid to education. By Charles Warren and J. L. M. Curry. pp. 99. (Circ. inf. 3, 1884.)

83. Proceedings of the Department of Superintendence of the National Educational Association, Washington, D. C., 1884. pp. 176. (Circ. inf. 4, 1884.)
   Partial contents: Supervision of public schools, by John W. Holcombe; Indian education, by J. M. Haworth; Indian education, by R. H. Pratt; Indian education, by S. C. Armstrong; Arbor day in the public schools, by J. B. Peaslee; Arbor day in the public schools, by B. G. Northrop; Recess, by W. T. Harris; No recess, by S. A. Ellis; How a State superintendent can best advance popular education, by E. E. Higbee; National aid for the support of public schools, by J. W. Dickinson; The educational status and needs of the South, by Robert Bingham; Legislation respecting national aid to education, proposed by the interstate educational convention, with remarks and tables; The new bill for national aid to public schools, by B. G. Northrop; Industrial education, by John M. Ordway; Public instruction in industrial pursuits, by A. P. Marble; Education at the World's Industrial and Cotton Centennial Exposition; The new order of Mercy, or Crime and its prevention, by George T. Angell; Education of the normal color sense, by B. Joy Jeffries; Supplementary reading, by George J. Luckey; Reading, by Chas. G. Edwards; Reading, by J. O. Wilson.
84. Suggestions respecting the educational exhibit at the New Orleans Exposition. 1884-85. pp. 28. (Circ. inf. 5, 1884.)
85. Rural schools. Progress in the past; means of improvement in the future. By Annie Tolman Smith. pp. 90. (Circ. inf. 6, 1884.)
86. Aims and methods of the teaching of physics. By Charles K. Wead. pp. 158. (Circ. inf. 7, 1884.)
87. City school systems in the United States. By John D. Philbrick. pp. 207. (Circ. inf. 1, 1885.)
88. Teachers' institutes. By James H. Smart. pp. 206. (Circ. inf. 2, 1885.)
89. Review of the reports of the British royal commissioner on technical instruction, with notes. By Chas O. Thompson. pp. 55. (Circ. inf. 3, 1885.)
90. Education in Japan. pp. 56. (Circ. inf. 4, 1885.)
91. Physical training in American colleges and universities. By Edward Mussey Hartwell. pp. 183. (Circ. inf. 5, 1885.)
92. Study of music in public schools. By Charles Warren. pp. 78. (Circ. inf. 1, 1886.)
93. Proceedings of the Department of Superintendence of the National Educational Association, Washington, D. C., 1886. pp. 91. (Circ. inf. 2, 1886)
   Partial contents: School superintendence a profession, by M. A. Newell; Duties of county superintendents, by D. L. Kieble; Reading circles for teachers, by Jerome Allen; The coeducation of the races, by Chas. S. Young; National aid to education, by J. A. Lovett; The education and religious interests of the colored people in the South, by S. M. Finger; Forestry in Education, by Warren Higley; Language work, by N. C. Dougherty; Growth and benefits of reading circles, by Herbert M. Skinner; City superintendence, by J. W. Akers; On the substitution of "Intermediate" for "Grammar" as a designation in the nomenclature of graded schools.
94. The college of William and Mary. By Herbert B. Adams. pp. 89. (Circ. inf. 1, 1887.)
95. Study of history in American colleges and universities. By Herbert B. Adams. pp. 299. (Circ. inf. 2, 1887.)
96. Proceedings of the Department of Superintendence of the National Educational Association, Washington, D. C., 1887. pp. 200. (Circ. inf. 3, 1887.)
   Partial contents: Public education on the Pacific coast, by F. M. Campbell; The examination and certification of teachers, by Andrew J. Rickoff, and report of committee on; Civil service and public schools: I, by Le Roy D. Brown, II, by Thomas P. Ballard; Powers and duties of school officers and teachers: I, by A. P. Marble, II, by J. M. Green; The best system of county and city supervision, by E. E. Higbee; Industrial education in our public schools: I, by F. W. Parker, II, by W. B. Powell; The province of the public school, by J. W. Dickinson; What a small city is doing in industrial education, by H. W. Compton; A system of grading for country schools, by J. W. Holcombe; The best system of State school supervision, by Warren Easton; State text-books, by F. M. Campbell; The nation and the public schools, by H. W. Blair; Education in Alaska, by Sheldon Jackson.
97. Thomas Jefferson and the University of Virginia. By Herbert B. Adams. pp. 308. (Circ. inf. 1, 1888)
98. History of education in North Carolina. By Charles Lee Smith. pp. 180. (Circ. inf. 2, 1888.)
99. History of higher education in South Carolina. By C. Meriwether. pp. 247. (Circ. inf. 3, 1888.)
100. Education in Georgia. By Chas. Edgeworth Jones. pp. 154. (Circ. inf. 4, 1888.)
101. Industrial education in the South. By A. D. Mayo. pp. 60. (Circ. inf. 5, 1888.)
102. Proceedings of the Department of Superintendence of the National Educational Association, Washington, D. C., 1888. pp. 165. (Circ. inf. 6, 1888.)
   Partial contents: How and to what extent can manual training be ingrafted on our system of public schools? by Chas. H. Ham. Discussed by A. P. Marble, Nicholas Murray Butler, H. H. Belfield, M. A. Newell, Chas. H. Ham; What is the purpose of county institutes, and how is it best secured? by Jessie B. Thayer; Elocution: Its place in education, by Martha Fleming; How shall the qualifications of teachers be determined? by A. S. Draper; Are the

PUBLICATIONS OF THE BUREAU OF EDUCATION. 1825

normal schools as they exist in our several States adequate to accomp'lsh the work for which they were established? by J. P. Wickersham. Discussed by J. W. Dickinson, Jerome Allen, Edward Brooks, and A. G. Boyden; Moral education in the common schools, by William T. Harris; Can school programmes be shortened and enriched? by Charles W. Eliot; Alaska, by N. H. R. Dawson; The relation of the superintendent and the teacher to the school, by A. E. Winship; National aid to education.

103. History of education in Florida. By George Gary Bush. pp. 54. (Circ. inf. 7, 1888.)
104. Report on school architecture and plans for graded schools. pp. 136. (Reprinted from Annual Report, 1868.)
105. Suggestions for a free-school policy for United States land grantees. pp. 6. 1872.
106. Statement of the theory of education in the United States, approved by many leading educators. pp. 22.- 1874.
107. National Bureau of Education; its history, work, and limitations. By Alexander Shiras. pp. 16. 1875.
108. Educational conventions and anniversaries, 1876. pp. 187.
109. International conference on education, held in Philadelphia in connection with the International Exhibition of 1876. pp. 92. 1879.
110. List of public-school officials in the States and Territories of the United States, 1875. pp. 62. 1875.
111. Manual of common native trees of the Northern United States. pp. 23. 1877.
112. Are the Indians dying out? By S. N. Clark. pp. 36. 1877.
113. International educational congress to be held at Brussels, Belgium, August, 1880. pp. 10. 1880.
114. Indian school at Carlisle barracks. pp. 5. 1880.
115. Industrial education in Europe. pp. 9. 1880.
116. Vacation colonies for sickly school children. pp. 4. 1880.
117. Progress of western education in China and Siam. pp. 13. 1880.
118. Educational tours in France. pp. 4. 1880.
119. Medical colleges in the United States. pp. 3. 1881.
120. Comparative statistics of elementary education in 50 principal countries. (Folding sheet.) 1881.
121. Fifty years of freedom in Belgium; Education in Malta; Third international geographical congress at Venice, 1881; Illiteracy and crime in France; School savings banks; Education in Sheffield. pp. 8. 1881.
122. Organization and management of public libraries. By William F. Poole. (Reprint from Pub. Librs. in the U. S. A., 1876.)
123. Library aids. By Samuel Green. pp. 10. 1881.
124. Recognized medical colleges in the United States. pp. 4. 1881.
125. Discipline of the school. By Hiram Orcutt. pp. 15. 1881. (Reprint of Circ. of information, November, 1871.)
126. Education and crime. By J. P. Wickersham. pp. 10. 1881.
127. Instruction in morals and civil government. By A. Vessiot. pp. 4. 1882.
128. Comparative statistics of elementary, secondary, and superior education in 60 principal countries. 1880. (Folding sheet.)
129. National pedagogic congress of Spain. pp. 4. 1882.
130. Natural science in secondary schools. By F. Mühlberg. pp. 9. 1882.
131. High schools for girls in Sweden. pp. 6. 1882.
132. Buffalini prize. pp. 5. 1883.
133. Education in Italy and Greece. pp. 8. 1883.
134. Answers to inquiries about the United States Bureau of Education. By Charles Warren. pp. 29. 1883.
135. Planting trees in school grounds. By Franklin B. Hough. pp. 8. 1883.
136. Southern Exposition of 1883-84, Louisville, Ky. (Two pamphlets relating to the exhibit of the United States Bureau of Education.) pp. 17. 1883. pp. 7. 1884.
137. Preliminary circular respecting the exhibition of education at the World's Industrial and Cotton Centennial Exposition. pp. 11. 1884.
138. Report of the director of the American School of Classical Studies at Athens for the year 1882-83. By Wm. W. Goodwin. pp. 13. 1884.
139. Building for the children of the South. By A. D. Mayo. pp. 16. 1884.
140. Statistics regarding the national aid to education. pp. 3. 1885.
141. Planting trees in school grounds, and celebration of Arbor Day. By Franklin B. Hough, and John B. Peaslee. pp. 8 + 64. 1885.
142. International educational congress at Havre. pp. 6. 1885.
143. Statistics of public libraries in the United States. pp. 98. 1886. (Reprinted from Annual Report 1884-85.)
144. Technical instruction. Special report, 1869. pp. 33 + 784. 8°. Washington (1870).
    Note.—First edition incomplete, printed pursuant to a call of House of Representatives, January 19, 1870. Second edition published as Volume XXI, of Barnard's Journal of Education. pp. 807.

145. Contributions to the annals of medical progress and medical education in the United States before and during the War of Independence. By Joseph M. Toner. pp. 118. 8°. Washington, 1874.
146. Historical sketch of Mount Holyoke Seminary. By Mary O. Nutting. Edited by F. B. Hough. pp. 24. 12°. [Washington, 1876.
147. Historical sketch of Union College. By F. B. Hough. pp. 81. 8°. Washington, 1876.
148. Public libraries in the United States of America, their history, condition, and management. Part I. Edited by S. R. Warren and S. N. Clark. pp. xxxv + 1187. Rules for a printed dictionary catalogue; Part II. By C. A. Cutter. pp. 89. 8°. Washington, 1876.
149. Contributions to the history of medical education and medical institutions in the United States of America, 1776-1876. By S. N. Davis. pp. 60. 8°. Washington, 1877.
150. Sketch of the Philadelphia Normal School for Girls. pp. 37. 8°. Washington, 1882.
151. Historical sketches of the universities and colleges of the United States. Edited by F. B. Hough. (History of the University of Missouri.) pp. 72. 8°. Washington, 1883.
152. Industrial education in the United States. pp. 319. 8°. Washington, 1883.
153. Art and industry.—Industrial and high art education in the United States. By I. Edwards Clarke. Part I. Drawing in the public schools. pp. cclix + 842. Washington, 1885.
 Note.—There are two other editions, with slightly varying titles; one ordered by the Senate, the other by Congress.
154. Outlines for a museum of anatomy. By R. W. Shufeldt. pp. 65. 8°. Washington, 1885.
155. Educational exhibits and conventions at the World's Industrial and Cotton Centennial Exposition, New Orleans, 1884-85. pp. 662. Foot pagination. 8°. Washington, 1886.
 Contents: Pt. I. Catalogue of exhibits. pp. 240. Pt. II. Proceedings of the International Congress of Educators. pp. 575. Pt. III. Proceedings of the Department of Superintendence of the National Educational Association, and addresses delivered on Education Days. pp. 148. New Orleans, 1885.
156. Indian education and civilization. Prepared in answer to Senate resolution of February 23, 1885. By Alice C. Fletcher, under direction of the Commissioner of Education. pp. 693. (Senate Ex. Doc. No. 95. Forty-eighth Congress, second session.)
157. Higher education in Wisconsin. By Wm. F. Allen and David E. Spencer. pp. 168. (Circ. inf. 1, 1889.)
158. Rules for a dictionary catalogue. By C. A. Cutter. pp. 33. 1st ed., Pt. II of public libraries in the United States, with corrections and additions. (Spec. rep., 1876.)
159. Indian education. By T. J. Morgan. pp. 28. (Bulletin 1, 1889.)
160. Proceedings of Department of Superintendence of the National Educational Association. Washington, March, 1889. pp. 300. (Circ. inf. 2, 1889.)
 Partial contents: Training of teachers: Psychology in its relation to pedagogy, by Nicholas Murray Butler; City training and practice schools, by W. S. Jackman; Purpose and means of city training schools, by S. S. Parr; County institutes, by Albert G. Lane; State teachers' institutes, by John W. Dickinson; Manual training, its relation to body and mind, by C. M. Woodward; The psychology of manual training, by W. T. Harris; Educational value of manual training, by Geo. P. Brown; The work of the city superintendent, by T. M. Balliet; The school principal, by George Holland; Teachers' examinations, by M. A. Newell; The State and higher education, by Fred. M. Campbell, Herbert B. Adams; Education in the South, by W. R. Garrett; National aid to education, by H. W. Blair.
161. History of Federal and State aid to higher education in the United States. By Frank W. Blackmar. pp. 348. (Circ. inf. 1, 1890.)
162. Rules for a dictionary catalog. By C. A. Cutter. 2d ed. of Pt. II of pub. libs. in the U. S., with corrections. pp. 133. 2d ed. (Spec. rep., 1889.)
163. History of education in Alabama, 1702-1889. By Willis G. Clark. pp. 281. (Circ. inf. 3, 1889.)
164. Honorary degrees as conferred in American colleges. By Charles Foster Smith. No. 1. 1890. pp. 12. (Misc. pub. or bulletin.)
165. English-Eskimo, and Eskimo-English vocabularies. Compiled by Roger Wells, jr., and John W. Kelly. pp. 72. (Circ. inf. 2, 1890.)
166. Rules and regulations for the conduct of schools and education in the Dist. of Alaska. pp. 7. (Misc. pub. 1890.)
167. Teaching and history of mathematics in the United States. By Florian Cajori. pp. 400. (Circ. inf. 3, 1890.)
168. Annual statement of the Commissioner of Education to the Secretary of the Interior. 1890. pp. 17. (Misc. pub. 1890.)
169. Preliminary report of the general agent of education for Alaska to the Commissioner of Education.—Introduction of Reindeer into Alaska. By Sheldon Jackson. pp. 15. (Misc. pub. 1890.)
170. Higher education in Indiana. By James Albert Woodburn. pp. 203. (Circ. inf. 1, 1891.)
171. Fourth International Prison Congress, St. Petersburg, Russia. By C. D. Randall. pp. 253. (Circ. 2, 1891.)
172. Rules for a dictionary catalog. By C. A. Cutter. 3d. ed., Pt. II of pub. libs. in the United States, with corrections and additions, and an alphabetical index. pp. 140. (Spec. rep., 1891.)
173. Sanitary conditions of schoolhouses. By Albert P. Marble. 1 p. 123. (Circ. 3, 1891.)

PUBLICATIONS OF THE BUREAU OF EDUCATION. 1827

174. History of higher education in Michigan. By Andrew C. McLaughlin. pp. 179. (Circ. inf. 4, 1891.)
175. History of higher education in Ohio. By Geo. W. Knight and John R. Commons. pp. 258. (Circ. inf. 5, 1891.)
176. History of higher education in Massachusetts. By Geo. Gary Bush. pp. 445. (Circ. inf. 6, 1891.)
177. Promotions and examinations in graded schools. By Emerson E. White. pp. 64. (Circ. inf. 7, 1891.)
178. Rise and growth of the normal school idea in the United States. By J. P. Gordy. pp. 145. (Circ. inf. 8, 1891.)
179. Biological teaching in the colleges of the United States. By John P. Campbell. pp. 188. (Circ. inf. 9, 1891.)
180. Annual statement of the Commissioner of Education to the Secretary of the Interior, 1891. pp. 21. (Misc. pub. 1891.)
181. Annual Report of the Commissioner of Education, 1888-89. Vol. I. pp. lix+669.
182. Same. Vol. II. pp. vi+671-1669.
183. Part I of the Report of the Commissioner of Education for the year 1888-89, with the Commissioner's introduction, and the contents of Parts I, II, and III. Special editions. pp. 274. (Spec. rep. 1891.)
184. Report of the general agent of education in Alaska for the year 1883-89. (Reprinted from Report of Commr. of Ed. for 1888-89. pp. 1245-1300.) (Misc. pub. 1891.)
185. Publications of the U. S. Bureau of Education from 1867-1890, with subject index. (Reprinted from An. Rep. of Commr. of Ed. for 1888-89. pp. 1453-1551.) (Misc. pub. 1891.)
186. Southern women in the recent educational movement in the South. By A. D. Mayo. pp. 300. (Circ. inf. 1, 1892.)
187. Analytical index to Barnard's American Journal of Education. 31 vols. 1855-1881. (Spec. rep. 1892.)
188. Benjamin Franklin and the University of Pennsylvania. By Franklin Newton Thorpe. pp. 450 (Circ. inf. 2, 1892.)
189. Annual statement of the Commissioner of Education to the Secretary of the Interior, 1892. pp. 21. (Misc. pub. 1892.)
190. Report on legal education. Prepared by committee of the American Bar Association, and the U. S. Bureau of Education. pp. 207. (Spec. rep. 1893.)
191. Education in Alaska, 1889-90. By Sheldon Jackson. (Reprint of chapter xvii of the report of the Commissioner of Education for 1889-90. pp. 45-1300.) (Misc. pub. 1893.)
192. Shorthand instruction and practice. By Julius E. Rockwell. pp. 206. (Circ. inf. 1, 1893.)
193. History of education in Connecticut. By Bernard C. Steiner. Contributions to American educational history, No. 14. pp. 300. (Circ. inf. 2, 1893.)
194. History of education in Delaware. By Lyman P. Powell. pp. 186. (Circ. inf. 3, 1893.)
195. Abnormal man; being essays on education and crime and related subjects, with digests of literature and a bibliography. By Arthur MacDonald. pp. 445. (Circ. inf. 4, 1893.)
196. Higher education in Tennessee. By Lucius Salisbury Merriam. Contributions to American educational history, No. 16. pp. 287. (Circ. inf. 5, 1893.)
197. Higher education in Iowa. By Leonard F. Parker. Contributions to American educational history, No. 17. pp. 190. (Circ. inf. 6, 1893.)
198. Annual Report of Commissioner of Education, 1889-90. Vol. I. xxvii+601.
199. Same. Vol. II. pp. vii+603-1724.
200. Catalog. of A. L. A. Library; 5,000 volumes for a popular library. pp. 592. (Spec. rep. 1893.)
201. Statistics of public libraries in the United States and Canada. By Weston Flint. pp. 213. (Circ. inf. 7, 1893.)
202. Spelling reform. By Francis A. March. A revision and enlargement of the author's pamphlet, published by the U. S. Bureau of Education, in 1881. pp. 86. (Circ. inf. 8, 1893.)
203. Education in Alaska, 1890-91. By Sheldon Jackson. pp. 923-960. (From An. Rept. Commr. of Education, 1890-91.) (Misc. pub. 1893.)
204. Annual statement of Commissioner of Education to Secretary of the Interior, 1893. By W. T. Harris. pp. 25.
205. Report of the committee on secondary school studies, appointed at the meeting of Nat. Ed. Ass., July 9, 1892, with the reports of the conferences, arranged by this committee, and held Dec. 28-30, 1892. pp. 249. (Spec. rep. 1893.)
206. Education in southwestern Virginia. By A. D. Mayo. (Reprint of chapter xxiv An. Rept. of Commissioner, 1890-91. pp. 881-921.)
207. Annual Report of Commissioner of Education, 1890-91. Vol. I. pp. xxx+654.
208. Same. Vol. II. pp. v+605-1549.
209. History of education in Rhode Island. By William Howe Tolman. pp. 210. Contributions Am. ed'l hist. No. 18. (Circ. inf. 1, 1894.)
210. History of higher education in Maryland. By Bernard C. Steiner. pp. 331. Contributions to Am. ed'l hist. No. 19. (Circ. of inf. 2, 1894.)
211. Annual Report of Commissioner of Education, 1891-92. Vol. I. pp. xxviii+636.
212. Same. Vol. II. pp. v+637-1294.

EDUCATION REPORT, 1894-95.

213. Annual statement of the Commissioner of Education to the Secretary of the Interior, 1894. By W. T. Harris. pp. 29. (Misc. pub. 1894.)
214. Education in Alaska. By Sheldon Jackson. pp. 873–892. (Reprinted from An. Rept. of Commr. of Edu., 1891-92.) (Misc. pub. 1894.)
215. Introduction of domesticated reindeer into Alaska, with maps and illustrations. By Sheldon Jackson. pp. 187. (Reprint of Senate Executive Document No. 70, 53d Congress, second session.) (Misc. pub. 1894.)
216. Art and industry. Education in the industrial and fine arts in the United States. By Isaac Edwards Clarke. Part II. Industrial and manual training in public schools. pp. cxlviii+1338. 8°. Washington, 1892.
217. Annual Report of Commissioner of Education, 1892-93. Vol. I. pp. ix+1224.
218. Same. Vol. II. pp. v+1225-2153.
219. Annual statement of the Commissioner of Education to the Secretary of the Interior, 1895. pp. 27.
220. Education in Alaska, 1892-93. By Sheldon Jackson. (From. An. Rept. of Commissioner of Education, 1892-93. pp. 705-1795.)
221. Annual Report of Commissioner of Education, 1893-94. Vol. I.
222. Same. Vol. II.
223. Education at the World's Columbian Exposition (1893), including reports and comments by American and foreign educators and delegates. (Reprinted from An. Rep. 1892-93. pp. 423-690.) 1896.
224. Papers prepared for the World's Library Congress held at the Columbian Exposition. Ed. by Melvil Dewey. pp. 691-1014. (Reprinted from An. Rep. 1892-93, Chap. IX.)
300. Our schools and our forests. By Franklin B. Hough. Address before Dept. of Superintendence Nat. Ed. Assoc., 1881. pp. 18. (Reprint from Circ. inf. 3, 1881.) (Mis. pub. 1881.)
301. Manual training. By C. M. Woodward. (Circ. inf. 2, 1889.)
302. Class intervals in city public schools. By James C. Boykin. pp. 3. (Misc. pub. 1893.)
303. What is education? Opinions of eminent men. pp. 16. (Misc. pub. 1870.)
304. Proceedings of the Dept. of Superintendence of the National Educational Association respecting State and city school reports. pp. 26. (Misc. pub. 1874.)
305. Industrial status and needs of the New South. By Robert Bingham. pp. 21. Delivered before the Dept. of Superintendence of the Nat. Ed. Assoc., February, 1884. (Misc. pub. 1884.)
306. Needs of education in the South. By Gustavus G. Orr. pp. 13. Delivered before the Dept. of Superintendence of the Nat'l Ed. Assoc., 1879. (Misc. pub. 1879.)
307. National aid to education. By John Eaton. Delivered before the Department of Superintendence of the Nat. Ed. Assoc., 1877. pp. 37. (Misc. pub. 1879.)
308. Needs of the Bureau of Education. By John Eaton. Delivered before Dept. of Superintendence of Nat'l Ed. Assoc., 1881. pp. 12. (Misc. pub. 1881.)
309. Museums illustrative of education. By John Eaton. Delivered before Dept. of Superintendence of Nat. Ed. Assoc., 1881. pp. 12. (Misc. pub. 1881.)
310. The World's Columbian Exposition, department of liberal arts. Circular No. 2. The educational exhibit at the World's Columbian Exposition. pp. 10. (Misc. pub. —.)
311. World's Columbian Exposition, department of liberal arts. Circ. No. 4. The educational exhibit No. 2. Statistics by graphic methods. Wing frames; State maps. Display of school statistics. pp. 17. (Misc. pub. —.)
312. United States Bureau of Education, an office in the Interior Department, 1867-1888. Commissioners: Henry Barnard, 1867-1870; John Eaton, 1870-1886; Nathaniel H. R. Dawson, 1886-1889. (Misc. pub. —.)
313. Technical education and industrial drawing. By Prof. Walter Smith. Delivered before the Dept. of Superintendence of Nat. Ed. Assoc., 1879. pp. 24. (Misc. pub. 1879.)
314. National schools of science, report on, by D. C. Gilman. pp. 20. (Reprinted from An. Rep. of U. S. Commissioner of Education for 1871. pp. 427-444.) (Misc. pub. 1872.)
315. Colleges and collegiate institutions in the United States. Statistics. pp. 11. (1871.)
316. International Exhibition, Philadelphia, 1876. Collections to illustrate the history of colleges, universities, professional schools, and schools of science. (1875.)
317. Prospectus of report of the Commissioner of Education for 1875. p. 1. 1875.
318. Chilean International Exposition of 1875, to be held at Santiago (educational programme). pp. 9. 1875.
319. Synopsis of proposed centennial; history of American education, 1776 to 1876. pp. 18. 1875.
320. Study of Anglo-Saxon. By F. A. March. pp. 10. (From An. Rep. 1876.)
321. Latin pronunciation. By W. G. Richardson. pp. 484-497. (From An. Rep. 1876.)
322. Pronunciation of Greek in this country. By James R. Boise. pp. 430-483. (From An. Rep. 1876.)
323. Education at the Paris Exposition, 1879. pp. 9. (From Circ. inf. 2, 1879.)
324. Sale of diplomas. pp. 4. 1880.
325. Report on education in Alaska, with maps and illustrations. By Sheldon Jackson. pp. 89. 1886.
326. Bureau of Education. Ohio Valley and Central States Centennial Exposition, July 4 to October 28, 1888. Exhibit of the Bureau. Compiled by John W. Holcombe. (Folding sheet.) pp. 8. 16°.
327. Annual statement of the Commissioner of Education to the Secretary of the Interior; being Introductory chapter of the An. Rep. 1888-89. By N. H. R. Dawson. pp. 28.
329. Report of the Commissioner of Education to the Secretary of the Interior, 1887. pp. 26. 1887.

CHAPTER XLVIII.
SCIENTIFIC TEMPERANCE INSTRUCTION IN THE PUBLIC SCHOOLS.

[Communicated by ALBERT H. PLUMB to the Boston Transcript, May 2, 1896.]

The spring meeting of the New England Conference of Educational Workers in Boston on the 25th instant drew together quite a number of prominent teachers and experts in the science of pedagogy. Superintendent Seaver gave fitting introduction to the speakers. His honor the mayor made an interesting and encouraging address on the way to secure improved sanitation in our schools. Much useful information was imparted by Dr. Durgin, of the board of health, and Dr. Hartwell, who has charge of physical culture in the city schools, and by other speakers. One of these, however, laid down a principle which is violently at war with the enlightened policy and efficient practice of our honored school authorities in this State and through the country. It was a principle which, if carried out according to the obvious intention of the speaker, would sweep away at once the greater part of the scientific temperance instruction now required by law in forty-one States, and in all schools under national control, as at Annapolis and at West Point. The falsity of this principle was at once exposed by a few words from Mrs. Mary H. Hunt, herself an educational authority, and, more than any other person living, personally in touch with educational and legislative authorities on this subject.

As there was no time, however, for any adequate discussion of the topic, it seems desirable that so vicious a principle be held up more definitely to the public view.

It was indeed well said, by the speaker referred to, that the moral attitude of the scholar in regard to conduct is the strong factor in securing right living; that the effort should be to raise the child to the plane where he chooses what is right; though it would have been more accurate to say, the moral attitude is the chief constituent of right living, for the moral attitude includes the choice of the right which is the effect, and not the cause concerning which we are inquiring. And to induce a pupil to take the right moral attitude, to choose the right, is a matter of exceeding difficulty and of indefinite progress—a progress which it is hard to mark. It depends largely on the personal character and influence of the teacher. It is not a matter which can be definitely ordered and supervised by the school authorities, and how far in each case the moral attitude of the pupil has yielded to the teacher's moral exhortation is uncertain. This is not the case in the work of imparting information. The school authorities can order that the teacher impart to the scholar certain definite scientific knowledge—truths and facts—and the teacher can so obey this order as to be sure that the pupil has a clear and thorough apprehension of them. They are his permanent possession thenceforth, and on active force necessarily and always in influencing his life. He may resist that influence. As the speaker intimated, information concerning the evil effects of intoxicants may lead boys to try the experiment of using liquor, to see the effects, and therefore he would draw the foolish inference that such information should be withheld. " Where ignorance is bliss it is folly to be wise" is a good motto indeed as to the experimental knowledge of vice, but not at all as to the scientific and theoretic knowledge of it.

1829

So that when the speaker inquires: "Does information guard against wrong conduct?" and in reply lays down the proposition that information is not a strong factor in promoting right living, he plants himself squarely in opposition to the great principles on which the educators and moralists of the land have established what is known and lauded the world over as the "American educational system of prevention of intemperance," viz, the early instruction by law of all pupils in the public schools upon the nature and effects of alcoholic drinks.

There are three manifest reasons why his position is untenable:

(1) It is opposed to the eternal law that truth has an inherent, impelling force. The moral nature of man has been so constituted by the God of truth that it is impossible to lodge in the human apprehension any proposition, any truth or fact, having any bearing on conduct—and nearly all truth, even philosophical and mathematical truth, has such a bearing, direct or indirect, near or remote—without more or less awakening of the sensibilities in regard to that moral bearing, more or less impulse upon the will toward the choice of the right.

(2) Authority as well as reason is against the position that information is not a strong factor in promoting right conduct. Indeed, the Great Teacher himself is explicitly against this position. "Sanctify them through Thy truth; Thy word is truth." And this affirmation is not limited to religious truth. There are a thousand declarations in God's word which are of the nature of philosophical propositions, or statements of historic fact, or of prudential maxims for worldly success, yet they may have an elevating power, e. g.: "The entrance of Thy words giveth light." "My people are destroyed for lack of knowledge." "He that ruleth his spirit is better than he that taketh a city." "The truth shall make you free." And upon the specific matter under consideration multitudes of educational experts have united in securing the legally enforced instruction precisely because of its moral preventive force. Who is higher authority than Dr. William T. Harris, United States Commissioner of Education? And his opinion was not long ago given in the Pall Mall Gazette, London, in these words:

"Instruction in what is called scientific temperance, conducted as it is under the laws of nearly all the States in the public elementary schools, furnishes a permanent and active means for the dissemination of correct views regarding the effect of intoxicating drinks upon the human body. All pupils will have their attention called to the subject every year, and intelligent pupils will understand with some degree of clearness the results of scientific investigation in this matter. Even the dull pupils who fail to seize the scientific points will carry away an impression in their minds that intoxicating drinks are very dangerous and should not be used even in moderate quantities. * * * Such instruction, too, is sure to furnish the greater portion of the intelligent pupils in schools with a correct scientific notion with regard to the investigations which have furnished the evidence for these conclusions.

"The utter destruction to the body and mind which comes from habitual intemperance, and the danger of moderate drinking in arousing an abnormal appetite for intoxicating liquors, will certainly be seen and understood by the great mass of pupils that attend the public schools. For this reason I do not see how anyone can question the great general usefulness of this scientific temperance instruction, established by law in most of the States of this nation. It may be said that this movement is the most effective one ever devised by the friends of temperance to abate a great evil, perhaps the greatest evil abroad in the land."

(3) Experience joins with reason and authority in condemning this depreciation of the moral effect of early acquaintance with scientific truth. In a number of States the laws requiring this instruction have been in force ten or fifteen years, and there is already a marked superiority in the morality of pupils coming from such teaching to enter collegiate and professional schools, according to the testimony of the faculties of such institutions. Young men have learned why every indulgence in dissipation is calculated to block their path to success, and they are less convivial

in their habits than those coming in former years. Even children now know too much to be caught by the cheap fallacies of tipplers. Take one instance from many. A millionaire brewer, a senator in another State, said to Mrs. Hunt, "I shall vote for your bill. I have sold out my brewery and am clean from the whole business. Let me tell you what occurred at my table. A guest was taken dangerously ill at dinner—insensible—and there was a call for brandy to restore him. My little boy at once exclaimed, 'No, that is just what he don't need. It will paralyze the nerves and muscles of the blood vessels so they will not send back the blood to the heart.' When the liquor was poured out to give the man, the lad insisted on pushing it back. 'You will kill him; he has too much blood in his head already.'" "How did you know all that?" his father afterwards asked. "Why, it is in my physiology at school." It seems the text-books, prepared by such men as Prof. H. Newell Martin, F. R. S., of Johns Hopkins University, had succeeded in giving the lad some definite information which was proving useful. "Senator," said Mrs. Hunt, "are you sorry your boy learned that at school?" "Madam," the man replied, raising his hand, "I would not take $5,000 for the assurance this gives me that my boy will never be a drunkard."

Information not a strong factor in controlling conduct? This kind of information is proving so strong a factor that the liquor dealers are alarmed and are combining in efforts to stop our schools from thus injuring their trade—an injury of which English owners of American brewery stock are complaining; and there are certain punctilious doctrinaires in science who appear more strenuous to preserve a certain theoretical precision in the order of succession of topics in the processes of instruction who seem more solicitous to spare the feelings and protect the self-indulgent tippling habits of the luxurious classes than to save the youth of the country from ruin by drink, who are combining with the brewers in endeavors, in different States just now, to repeal or embarrass and neutralize the enforcement of the temperance instruction laws.

The agents of the brewers in various States are repeating over and over these same hostile arguments which were heard here at the meeting on Saturday last, alleging the inefficacy of such instruction, as if they desired its efficacy, and claiming that it is impossible for the young before they reach college—or certainly previous to entering the high school—to attain any scientific knowledge on these subjects, a rule which would deny to 95 per cent of our school children, who never reach the high school, all definite scientific instruction on these topics, limiting them to occasional moral exhortations by their teachers.

It is contended that it is out of the due order to touch on these subjects until a pupil has thoroughly mastered the science of chemistry and the philosophy of nutrition. What if it is? What valuable interests will suffer if, on account of a great and appalling moral exigency, these all-important practical themes are taken up in advance, since they must be taken up then in 95 per cent of the cases, if attended to at all? At any rate, the people of this country, the parents of our school children, have decided that they shall be thus taken up, because they are determined to use every possible endeavor to protect their children from the awful dangers of intoxicating drinks. And how utterly wrongheaded, and cold-hearted, too, it is for teachers, who are the servants of the people, or for anyone else, to interfere with this great philanthropic movement, which has cost untold sacrifices of time and toil to establish, and on which the future welfare of the nation largely depends!

Doubtless the bulk of our school teachers are not yet equal to our most learned physicians in their physiological attainments, but to despise, therefore, and to decry as unsound, misleading, and morally worthless such instruction as they are able to give on these subjects, is to show recklessness in regard to facts, and indifference in regard to the evils which correct teaching is calculated to prevent, for these evils are so dire and threatening that all wise minds must resolve to use, instantly and incessantly, such preventive means as we have, rather than to postpone all effort to that indefinite future when means sufficiently perfect to satisfy these extremists shall be provided. Meanwhile it is encouraging to know that the trustees of the new American University at Washington have already taken measures, in response to the request of friends of this instruction, to establish there a College of Scientific Temperance, not as a propaganda, but for original research, and for the training of the "teachers of teachers" on these themes, which the perils of national life in Europe and America are pressing to the front.

The unworthy methods which nearly everywhere mark the opposition to this temperance instruction deserve strong rebuke. Have the distinguished authors of the temperance text-books—some of them known and honored as scientific authorities on two hemispheres—told lies in their books? If so, why does not someone point out the lies? If not, then reputable men should have done with the continual and contemptible insinuation that our children are learning in school what they will have to unlearn in life.

The misrepresentations made in the progress of the recent great contest in New York have been shameful, but all in vain, for by overwhelming majorities last week the house and senate passed the improved law, demanded by the representatives of over 1,000,000 members of churches and other philanthropic bodies in the State. Certainly the victories which are continually attending this hard-pressed conflict are so remarkable as to warrant a reverent conviction that the especial favor of Providence is attending a movement which, in its inception and prosecution, has been largely imbued with a spirit of prayer, which is purely philanthropic, which is accordant with true wisdom and scientific truth, and which, in its wide extent and confessed potency for good, is by far the most promising of all present measures for the prevention of vice.

TEMPERANCE INSTRUCTION IN PUBLIC SCHOOLS. 1833

TEMPERANCE EDUCATION MAP OF THE UNITED STATES AND TERRITORIES.

[Furnished to the Bureau by the Department of Scientific Temperance Instruction of the W. C. T. U., Mrs. Mary H. Hunt, superintendent. Utah was under the national temperance law until it became a State; since then no advice has been received regarding the enactment of a temperance education law.]

States in white have a temperance education law. Those in black have none.

EXPLANATION OF MARKS.

× The cross signifies that scientific temperance is a mandatory study in public schools.
* The star signifies that this is a mandatory study, and that a penalty is attached to the enforcing clause of this statute in the State or Territory to which it is affixed.
† The dagger signifies that the study is not only mandatory, but is required of all pupils in all schools.
‡ The double dagger signifies that the study is required of all pupils in all schools, and is to be pursued with text-books in the hands of pupils able to read.
‖ The parallel indicates that the study is to be taught in the same manner and as thoroughly as other required branches.
§ The section mark indicates that text-books on this topic used in primary and intermediate schools must give one-fourth or one-fifth their space to temperance matter, and those used in high schools not less than twenty pages.
¶ The paragraph indicates that no teacher who has not passed a satisfactory examination in this subject is granted a certificate or authorized to teach.
= Three lines indicate that text-books on this topic shall give full and adequate space to the temperance matter.

ED 95——58*

www.ingramcontent.com/pod-product-compliance
Lightning Source LLC
Chambersburg PA
CBHW020253090426
42735CB00010B/1898